I0823823

Jump Cuts

Essays on Surrealism, Film, Music, Culture, and Other Utopian Topics

Mark Polizzotti

The Song Cave

For my parents
and for Jacky

The Song Cave

www.the-song-cave.com

Author photo by Jacky Colliss Harvey
Design and layout by Janet Evans-Scanlon

ISBN: 979-8-9912988-3-4
Library of Congress Cataloguing-in-Publication Data has been applied for.

FIRST PRINTING

CONTENTS

Profound Occultation 1

Patabiographical 43

Love in Vain 49

Through a Glass, Amorously 68

A Child's Garden of Eccentricities 74

"Love and Theft": Dylan's Appropriations 86

The Complicated Little Girl 116

Which Year at Where? 126

Whoever Is with Me Is Against Me 133

Lives Behind Lives: Biography as Autobiography 147

Art of the Inane 155

Surrealism's Children 178

Jump Cuts 195

Acknowledgments 211

PROFOUND OCCULTATION

1. Gala Evenings

On the 24th of March 1924, the French poet Eugène-Paul Grindel, only slightly better known to the world as Paul Eluard, stood up from a café table to buy matches and failed to return. For the next six months, his closest companions would be left to wonder about his fate, their only clue a *pneumatique* Eluard had dispatched to his father threatening death to anyone who came after him.

Eluard's journey took him south to Marseilles, then by various steamers to Holland, Martinique, Tahiti, Java, New Guinea, New Zealand, Singapore, and Saigon, from where he would finally return to France in September. His friends, meanwhile, including the soon-to-be Surrealists André Breton and Louis Aragon, without even knowing to which latitudes Eluard had vanished, lost no time in reading his histrionic gesture as a reenactment of Rimbaud's drop-out to Ethiopia some fifty years earlier. In sailing to Indochina, Eluard was not, however, striking out as a gunrunner in an update of Rimbaud's mythic change of life, but simply taking a break from a very real, in some ways very banal, and at all events intolerable home situation. Much as generations of art critics, university professors, and museum curators would later do to the Surrealists' exploits, the future Surrealists themselves were already inflating their comrade's escapade, interpreting it to suit their own expectations, and fundamentally missing the point.

About two years earlier, in the summer of 1922, Eluard and his Russian-born wife, Helena Dmitrievna Diakonova, whom he'd nicknamed

Gala, had spent the summer in the Tyrol with the German painter Max Ernst and family. Eluard was already a great admirer of Ernst, and meeting him only cemented his devotion. Gala's attraction was much more visceral. Ernst, for his part, was awestruck by both the Olympian poet from Paris and the alluring creature at his side, who knew her own desires and didn't mince words. When the Eluards returned home several months later, Ernst tagged along, leaving his bride and young son (the future painter Jimmy Ernst) to fend for themselves in postwar Germany. He moved into the Eluard family home in the Paris suburbs, basking in the attentions of the poets and artists to whom Eluard introduced him and covering the house's inner and outer walls with murals proclaiming the trio's unorthodox living arrangements. The sexually uptight Breton remarked to his wife that one in particular, a huge nude of Gala, "surpasses in horror anything one could imagine." Eluard defended Ernst's works, straining relations with his good friend Breton.

Then in its sixth year, the Eluards' marriage had never been a model of exclusivity—Paul proudly showed off photos of his wife in the nude to all and sundry and, to Breton's disgust, virtually raised promiscuity to an art form—and at first the husband insisted that no sacrifice was too great for his "spiritual brother" Max, whom he "loved much more than he did Gala." The stresses were already starting to show, however. That same year, Eluard began his verse collection *Repetitions* with the lines "In a corner agile incest / Circles the virginity of a little dress"; the title of the poem is "Max Ernst." Still, regardless of their infidelities, Eluard's assumption had always been that, at the end of the day, Gala would remain his "darling little girl," and his alone. But Gala, an unrepentant materialist and master at trading up, was already loosening her conjugal bonds.

By the start of 1924, Eluard was feeling abandoned by his wife and thrown over by his friends, some of whom didn't bother suppressing their mirth at his expense. Breton's wife, Simone Kahn Breton, a more sympathetic witness, described Eluard bar-hopping every night, "throwing his money away, drunk, afraid to go to sleep alone." Eluard published the sad, alienated volume of poems *Dying from Not Dying*, which he dedicated to Breton as his "last book." As Robert McNab nicely puts it in *Ghost Ships: A Surrealist Love Triangle*,* his study of the Paul-Gala-Max ménage, Eluard

> indeed feared that these might be the last poems he would write, perhaps because he had felt so low for so long it seemed he would never again have anything uplifting to say. In contrast Ernst was on song and his inspiration constant, which Eluard could see better than anyone . . . His treasured friend had occupied every corner of his life, from the recesses of his imagination as a poet to the intimacy of his bedroom, from the front door of his home up to the attic . . . Eluard had given Ernst everything and now stood empty-handed, a hollow man.

Soon afterward, Eluard embezzled 17,000 francs from his father's real estate business and set off on his grand voyage.

Though a comparatively minor episode in the story of Surrealism, Eluard's journey, and the repercussions it had within his circle, adumbrate several of the key themes that would recur throughout the movement's history: the role of adventure and chance, sexual tension and experimentation, the mixture of politics and aesthetics. It also points up the latent conflict between the international reach of Surrealism and the fact that much of it was generated by, and firmly grounded in,

---

* Yale University Press, 2004.

the French capital. Finally, as an *acte gratuit*, it anticipates and mitigates Breton's later, more snarling definition of the "simplest Surrealist act" as firing blindly into a crowd of strangers.

Moreover, the ramifications of Eluard's adventure engage one of the more persistent fallacies to vex Surrealism, fostered over the years by countless exhibitions and coffee-table books: that it was primarily an art movement, buttressed by just enough theoretical and political rantings to keep professors happy. In the United States especially, this misconception seems to have the hardiness of crabgrass. While legend has preserved the daily café meetings, over which André Breton presided like the CEO of some avant-garde multinational, we tend to forget that the discussions only rarely concerned art per se.

The reality is that Surrealism began not as a visual movement but as a philosophical and, given its principal members, literary one—or rather, a movement of ideas that took the medium of words as its chief instrument. Although several visual artists were associated with the group from the outset, the plastic arts barely register in Breton's inaugural *Manifesto of Surrealism* of 1924. Driven by an urgent sense of self-exploration and an absolute non-conformism (a term the Surrealists were using well before it became a sixties cliché), Surrealism aimed at being a top-to-bottom refurbishing of human understanding, exposing the flashes of marvelous wonder hidden in the creases of everyday life. It was meant to engage—and to challenge—the way our minds structure the world through language, taking as its weapons automatic writing, verbal collage, sleep trances, and other spoken and written manifestations.

The status of the visual arts, on the other hand, was not n early so clear-cut. The Surrealist writer Pierre Naville tried to brush aside the entire notion early on by asserting that there was "no such thing as *Surrealist painting*." In rebuttal, Breton began examining the question more closely in his seminal essay *Surrealism and Painting* (1928), which sought to pinpoint the qualities that, in painting as in poetry, defined a work as Surrealist. The short answer—its ability to externalize a "*purely internal model*"—left the door open by extension to all forms of visual statement, including film and so-called "Surrealist objects" (Meret Oppenheim's fur-lined teacup being no doubt the most recognizable). The ambiguity was exacerbated by the fact that many of the Surrealists frequently blurred the line between genres: Dalí, Ernst, Magritte, and Carrington were also accomplished writers; Artaud, Desnos, and Breton created important plastic objects; and the poet Jacques Prévert became a well-known scenarist.

On the American continent, however, Surrealism has primarily gained a reputation as a visual school, with its writings accorded the secondary status of philosophical scaffolding or literary by-product. To some extent, this was predictable. For one thing, Surrealist paintings are easier to absorb than abstruse poems and tracts, and from the start pioneering museum and gallery curators such as Chick Austin, Julien Levy, and Alfred Barr brought them to our attention in ways that a would-be publisher of Surrealist verse could only have fantasized. Furthermore, many Surrealists, regardless of their chosen medium, have been closely involved with the art world—as dealers, critics, promoters, and gallerists, not to mention collectors. (Witness the extent of Breton's art holdings by the time of his death in 1966, and the furor when they were auctioned off in 2003.)

Another reason why the North American view of Surrealism has been so skewed is that we tend to misunderstand or insufficiently appreciate the environment from which it arose. The movement emerged at a particular historical moment (the aftermath of World War I), from under a particular cultural weight (the long legacy of Greco-Latin rationalism), and in a particular place (Paris, crucible of the avant-garde).

These circumstances were as central to its formation as the theories of Freud or the accidents that first brought together its principals, and it is as difficult to imagine Surrealism without them as it is to imagine Monty Python or The Beatles coming out of anywhere but 1960s England. But we North Americans don't see things in quite the same way. Our literature is fashioned from different spaces, both physical and psychological. Our own brand of expansive rebellion is quite distinct from Surrealism's compressed revolt against layer upon layer of social, behavioral, and artistic conditioning. It is not so much that the boundaries we set between art and life (or, for that matter, between the arts themselves) are more rigid than the ones the Surrealists labored to demolish, but rather that art and life seem to exist in wholly separate spheres.

Which is why books such as Robert McNab's *Ghost Ships*, with its focus on Eluard's seemingly negligible escapade, come closer to conveying the thrill and open-endedness of the Surrealist adventure than many a scholarly study. The latter category tends to focus on the, as it were, symptoms of Surrealism rather than its root cause, or on the moral and spiritual restlessness that underlay its productions and its stances. It is to McNab's credit that he has recognized and chosen to highlight an incident that, at the dawn of the movement proper, brings that primary malaise to the surface.

Among other things, McNab sets Eluard's journey, and its "reading" by his friends, within the broader context of Surrealist voyages. Many of these voyages were purely imaginary, circumscribed by the squares of paper on which their writing, automatic and otherwise, appeared. Breton, in his 1922 essay "The Mediums Enter," recorded the flights of fancy taken by members of the group during hypnotic stupors, what became known as the "sleeping fits" (on which, more later). These fits, akin to mediumistic trances, were prized by Breton and the other participants as doorways to a next level of consciousness and verbal expression. "We're living simultaneously in the present, the past, and the future," Simone Breton wrote to her cousin. "After each séance we're so dazed and broken that we swear never to start up again, and the next day all we can think about is putting ourselves back in that catastrophic atmosphere." The experiments came to an end after some of the participants started showing a toxic addiction to the nightly sessions, as well as frankly homicidal tendencies while under the influence.

Not all the Surrealists' travels were quite so virtual, of course. Breton and Aragon would sometimes prowl around the Buttes-Chaumont park late at night (their "Mesopotamia for half an hour," as Aragon wrote), or wander through the city streets in quest of what Breton called "petrifying coincidences." Prompted by Eluard's disappearance, they and two others also set off on a random excursion around the Sologne region of central France—a kind of automatic record composed with the feet—that ended, after ten days of minor revelations and increasingly frayed nerves, with Breton putting them all on a train home. Most of the time, however, these Marco Polos of the mind did not feel the need to venture outside the city confines. Breton in particular drew inspiration from Paris, deeming life anywhere else to be "artificial, like a stage set"; apart from an enforced wartime interlude in New York in the 1940s, he occupied his address at 42 Rue Fontaine, near Place Pigalle, continuously from 1922 until his death forty-four years later.

Eluard's own, less provincial exploration is, as McNab puts it, "ripe for treatment as a novel or a film," and the first several chapters of his book are packed with the stuff of old-fashioned adventure yarns: noble rivalries, beaux gestes, creaky steamers headed for exotic destinations, and gallons of local color. In keeping with the genre, there is even a dramatic reunion. In August, Gala and Max—who, unbeknownst to the others, had been in touch with Eluard for months—met up with the errant poet in Singapore, from where the trio moved on to Saigon. Several weeks later, Gala and Paul set sail for Marseilles, their wedding vows momentarily renewed, leaving Ernst to find his own way back. For both Eluard and Ernst, this last stop, in what was then French Indochina, proved the crux of the trip—in Eluard's case, because it marked his reconciliation with Gala, and in passing exposed the young middle-class scion to colonialism's more flagrant abuses; in Ernst's, because it provided a lexicon of imagery that would last him a lifetime.

The second half of *Ghost Ships* explores in detail how the temples of Angkor Wat and other monuments later resurfaced in many of Ernst's paintings, frottages, and decalcomanias. While the narrative from here on becomes less enthralling, McNab's discussion of the trip's influence on Ernst does make an intriguing art-historical point, and the author ably backs it up with illustrations juxtaposing artworks with photographs of the various sites. (Though perhaps more surprising are the Gauguin-like sketches that Ernst produced while in Indochina. Does foreign travel breed its own artistic style?) Even the painter's totemic alter ego Loplop, "the Bird Superior," turns out to be based on a garuda figure seen at Angkor Thom.

There is an emotional resonance to all this as well, which lifts these visual echoes above mere reminiscence. It was during the roughly two weeks he stayed behind after the Eluards' departure that the abandoned Ernst visited the Cambodian and Vietnamese monuments that later figured in his art; perhaps because of this, in almost every case these images, when they appear in his work, give off a sense of desolation and despair. The reality, which McNab underscores with a neat parallel, is that both men were in the same sad boat: "The *Goentoer* [the liner taken by the Eluards] was headed for the breaker's yard, as was the Eluards' marriage. There is an equally striking similarity between Max

Ernst and the vessel on which he returned to Europe . . . a battered steamer, the SS *Affon*, that had weathered many storms. Perhaps he identified with her, for the *Affon* was also on her way to the scrapheap, to which Gala had effectively consigned him."

Back in Paris by October 1924, Eluard faced up to his friends, who were shocked to see the myth so casually deflate into a man. "Eluard is back. No comments," Simone reported to her cousin. "I cannot forgive anyone for stealing my emotions. Still less André's . . . What is a creature compared to a symbol? 'Not dying from dying' . . . Now it's as if he never left." Eluard blithely dismissed the entire episode as "piffling" and joined in the launch of the Surrealist movement proper that same month. Still, the journey wasn't as inconsequential as he made out, for Eluard brought back a number of objects that helped focus the group's attention on non-Western art, a study that over the years would bear diversely flavorsome fruits. He also helped infuse Surrealism with a renewed sense of anti-colonial fervor, which in the 1920s and '30s (the movement's "heroic period," so-called) informed some of its most eloquent protests.

Gala, meanwhile, remained Mme. Eluard for the time being, having perhaps realized that her father-in-law's land developments provided a better standard of living than did her German lover's unsalable paintings. As for Ernst, while his relations with the "slithering, glittering creature" (as his discarded wife had characterized Gala) were more or less at an end, and while he no longer enjoyed a bed under the Eluards' roof, this did not mean he and the poet had fallen out—far from it. In the event, the two men's friendship long outlasted either one's relationship with the Russian femme fatale.

Eluard's relations with Gala continued in marital form for another five years, and in a less codified, though not exactly platonic, fashion nearly until his death a quarter-century later. His missives to her (collected in the 1980s as *Letters to Gala*) yield a fascinating epistolary history of Surrealism, and amply display the fanaticism that characterized Eluard's allegiances throughout his life. This kind of blinkered fealty—whether to Gala, Surrealism, or, later, Communism—fueled his flight to Saigon in the 1920s, his proselytizing as Breton's lieutenant in the 1930s, and his treacly odes to Stalin in the late '40s. (That's Eluard's quavering voice one hears intoning the words *"mon amour, mon amour"* on the soundtrack of the 1930 Dalí/Buñuel masterpiece *L'Age d'or*, and it speaks volumes.)

Such fanaticism also underlies the love poems in Eluard's superlative 1926 collection *Capital de la douleur*, known in English, though not well enough, as *Capital of Pain*. One of France's most notable poets, Eluard is also highly difficult to translate felicitously, and therefore has had relatively little exposure in this country. This is unfortunate, since his verse often scales the heights of what Surrealist poetry in its early phase could achieve, and in this regard *Capital of Pain* is quite possibly the movement's crowning jewel. When Godard needed a prototypical collection of Surrealist love verse for the heroine to read in his celluloid comic book *Alphaville* (1965), it was a battered copy of *Capital of Pain* he placed in Anna Karina's hands.

Capital of Pain actually comprises several collections, beginning with *Repetitions*, published around the start of the Ernst-Gala affair in 1922, and ending with a suite of "new poems" written mainly in 1925—in other words, the period recounted in *Ghost Ships*, which makes these poems an intriguing counterpoint to McNab's melodrama.* Not surprisingly, the range of emotions is vast, veering in the course of several pages from ardent desire

* Some, but not all, of these English versions are from Paul Eluard, *Capital of Pain*, trans. Mary Ann Caws, Patricia Terry, and Nancy Kline (Boston: Black Widow Press, 2006).

She is standing on my eyelids
And her hair mingles with mine,
She has the shape of my hands,
She has the color of my eyes

("A Woman in Love")

to a barely suppressed bitterness that strips off the veneer of equanimity Eluard showed to the outside world. Poems like "The Big Uninhabitable House" and "Caught in the Trap," or lines such as

Tears in the eyes, the sorrows of the sorrowful,
Dull sorrows, dreary tears.
He asks for nothing, he isn't unfeeling,
He's sad in prison and sad if he's free

("No Hard Feelings")

and

How can one enjoy everything?
Better to wipe it all out.
The man who moved in all directions,
Sacrificed everything, conquered everything

("In the Heart of My Love")

reveal the underbelly of Eluard's proclaimed fraternal devotions. One remarkable poem, "In the Flame of the Lash," is a startling piece of gleeful sadomasochism, almost obscene in its coupling of naked anger and self-abasement:

> Sure—hello to my face!
> Light chimes in great desires more clearly than scenery.
> Sure—hello to your harpoons,
> To your screams, to your leaps, what you keep hidden down below!
> I have lost, I have won, just look at what I've climbed upon.

These lines are strong drink, poured out by someone who was a lot more furious than he could afford to acknowledge, and their seething rage seems fiercer still by contrast with the forced bonhomie and resignation of so many other pieces in the collection (*"douleur"* being equal parts "pain" and "sorrow").

Despite his Surrealist trappings, Eluard is in some ways a very classical poet. Less intellectually thrilling than Breton, less verbally dazzling than Aragon, he preferred the solidity of poetic truths expressed with blunt affirmation, though that affirmation often turns hermetic: this is the world, these poems declare, but it is accessible only through us. While Breton went pearl diving into automatic writing and sleep trances, Eluard much more deliberately honed his verses, using startling juxtapositions and dream narratives—those Surrealist staples—to invest them with their distinctive aura. His lines, and perhaps nowhere more so than in *Capital of Pain*, are models of what French prosody can do once it lets its hair down and tosses the Académie rulebook into the Seine.

★

In July 1925, less than a year after his return from Southeast Asia, Max Ernst participated in an infamous banquet in honor of the poet Saint-Pol Roux, then had to absent himself from Paris after the evening erupted in a brawl: as an undocumented alien and one of the melee's instigators, Ernst was ripe for deportation. While holing up in a hotel in Brittany, he developed—or chanced upon—the technique of frottage, in which the textures produced by rubbing paper over various surfaces such as floorboards or walls yielded elements of fabulous landscapes. Ernst was attuned to the transformative potential of a wide variety of media, and the patterns he derived from the rough flooring of his hotel room—a modernist take on Leonardo's advice to his students to find their subjects by staring at an old façade—became a consistently fertile generator of his art.

As much as for his painting, in fact, Ernst is known for the breadth and inventiveness of his experiments with numerous techniques, including frottage, grattage (frottage's flip side, in which pigment is removed from a sheet placed atop an object), decalcomania (pulling two painted surfaces apart to create organic, drip-like patterns, such as in the masterful *Europe after the Rain* of 1940–42), photomontage, and especially collage, a lifelong pursuit and one that, for Ernst, was much more about mental interconnection than visual cut-and-paste. As he put it, "It's not the *colle* [glue] that makes the collage." The renowned Ernst specialist Werner Spies has stated that collage epitomizes Ernst's aesthetic. It certainly accounts for many of the oddly disquieting, disquietingly hilarious, or hilariously puzzling images and juxtapositions that run through Ernst's work, and that make him one of the most provocative and least dated of the Surrealist artists. In attitude alone, Ernst could still teach whippersnappers like Jeff Koons and Damien Hirst a thing or two.

It is primarily this Ernst, the artistic visionary rather than the hapless Romeo, whom we meet in *Max Ernst: A Retrospective*, the catalogue to the Metropolitan Museum's major exhibition from 2005. Compared with the Ernst portrayed in *Ghost Ships*, the one that emerges from the catalogue comes across as another artist altogether. Robert McNab's Ernst is all sorts of things: a flagrant opportunist, a feckless husband, a handsome charmer, a sexual swashbuckler hoisted on his own petard, and, of course, a brilliant and innovative artist; nowhere is he anything less than passionate, even if the steely crags of his intelligence and hawklike countenance could make him seem positively glacial.

The Ernst presented by the contributors to the Met catalogue, on the other hand, is a much more focused, directed, but in some ways two-dimensional creature. I'm tempted to ascribe this mainly to the conventions of the traditional exhibition catalogue and leave it at that; but before letting the editors entirely off the hook, it might be worth pausing for a moment over what this means. *Max Ernst: A Retrospective* offers many of the pluses and minuses of museum-produced books. On the plus side, there is a wealth of in-depth discussion by numerous learned authorities (six, in this case), each mining some vein of the work for whatever new interpretations can be teased out of it; pages of well-printed reproductions (the ones here look especially bright and sharp); a cursory but useful chronology that provides easy reference to the artist's milestones; and some valuable insights into the antecedents of Ernst's creations. On the minus side, there is a tendency to compartmentalize the work into digestible essay topics, and to view it through the borrowed lens of secondary and tertiary sources; to delve ever more deeply into Ernst's career as a producer of art while practically ignoring his activities as a Dadaist and Surrealist; and to couch it all—with a few exceptions, but only a few—in language that reeks of the lecture-hall.

To take one example: an essay called "Max Ernst and the Great Masters," by the German scholar and museum director Thomas

Gaehtgens, begins with the programmatic assertion, "Viewers can certainly explore the bizarre world of his pictures without knowing his models, but if they do, they will fail to appreciate the exciting creative process behind his inventions." This is reasonable enough as far as it goes, though it rests on the dubious assumption that only learned elucidation of an artist's approach and source materials can lead to a true understanding of their creative genius. Dr. Gaehtgens gives many interesting examples of how Ernst borrowed and distorted motifs, from a statue by Carpeaux that turns up in his 1929 collage novel *La Femme 100 têtes* (*The Hundred Headless Woman*) to a photograph by the Spanish muralist José Maria Sert that probably inspired the iconic (and still highly amusing) *Blessed Virgin Chastises the Infant Jesus before Three Witnesses: A.B., P.E., and the Artist.* He also, to his credit, notes that Ernst's relation to the Old Masters was determined by a "strong emotional response" rather than purely intellectual affinities. The problem—which the author seems to take as a feature rather than a bug—is that "Surrealist art has long since been integrated into the history of intellectual and cultural innovation in the twentieth century." In other words, Ernst, Dalí, Duchamp, Miró, Masson, and their peers are now artifacts of history, to be (as Breton put it in 1927, protesting a similar treatment of Lautréamont) "assigned a place between So-and-So and Such-and-Such."

Now, these painters *have* to some extent become artifacts of history, no use denying it. But to take them only as such, to reduce them—or any artist—to mere points on a curatorial timeline, is to sidestep the fundamental qualities that make them worth studying (or viewing) in the first place. Dr. Gaehtgens can tell me where Ernst found certain motifs for the collages of *La Femme 100 têtes.* What he can't tell me is why those collages still elicit a thrill every time I leaf through them; nor—and here's the real pity—does he ever evoke a sense of that thrill. (It is instructive in this regard to compare McNab's discussion of Indonesian visual elements in Ernst's work, which brings into play biographical and sociopolitical details alongside the artistic and architectural ones, and which paints a much more vibrant picture.)

I would be remiss not to mention one more essay in *Max Ernst*, by the historian Robert Storr, which takes as its focus Ernst's three collage novels, the other two being *Rêve d'une petite fille qui voulut entrer au Carmel* (1930; translated by Dorothea Tanning as *Dream of a Little Girl Who Wanted to Take the Veil*) and *Une semaine de bonté* (1934). Unlike the other pieces, Storr's essay is unabashedly personal, nearly as much about his own love of rare books as it is about Ernst's contributions to his library. Along the way, he nonetheless manages to lay bare many of the psychological, as well as artistic, underpinnings of Ernst's collages, including the artist's deep-seated ambivalence toward the "sexually assertive women"—avatars of Gala?—who populate many of these creations. He also zeroes in on the works' "alienating effect, which feeds on ambiguity," correctly identifying it as "Surrealism's basic, still intoxicating ingredient." As he notes, many of Ernst's collages convey a sense of the uncanny precisely because the disparate parts are stitched together so seamlessly, the fissures they conceal opening "not on the page but in the mind's eye." It is this mental vista that is too often given short shrift in critical studies, in favor of the kind of seeing—reassuringly coherent, yet so inadequate to the task—that Marcel Duchamp dismissed as "retinal."

★

By 1929, Ernst had married his second wife, a pure product of French Catholicism named Marie-Berthe Aurenche (no doubt his "little girl who wanted to take the veil"), and was stepping down his involvement in Surrealism's daily operations. That same year, the young Catalan painter Salvador Dalí, seeking to exploit the fame and fortune he'd already been garnering at home, arrived in the French capital, blundering into a Surrealist movement in full crisis: a number of its original members had stalked off or been thrown out, the wellsprings of automatic writing had seemingly run dry, and the group's overtures to the French Communist Party threatened to mire it in sectarian squabbles. Dalí, with his flagrantly idiosyncratic paintings and deliriously inventive critical fabulations, was a gust of fresh air. Although Breton would later make sport of him, with more than a tinge of bitterness, there is no question that for nearly a decade he saw Dalí as a source of badly needed renewal.

Dalí's introduction to the Surrealist group came via the art dealer Camille Goemans, who in the spring of 1929 bundled his young client off to a well-frequented soirée and thrust him at Paul Eluard. In the five years since his Asian adventure, Eluard had emerged as an influential poet and important art collector. He was now thirty-four; Dalí was nine years his junior, and, as Ernst had been before him, in awe. "Eluard struck me as a legendary being," Dalí later wrote. "He drank calmly, and appeared completely absorbed in looking at the beautiful women. Before we took leave of each other, he promised to come to see me the next summer at Cadaqués," where Dalí had a beach house.

In August, the Eluards did just that. To greet them properly, the Spaniard had togged himself out in a tattered shirt, a dubiously soiled Speedo, pearls, a jasmine flower, and laundry bluing, with a smear of goat dung for good measure. But a first glimpse of Gala's bare back from his bedroom window (as he later recounted) sent a shock through his system that neutralized his interest in all such artifices. Over the following days, Dalí and his "sister soul" established a relationship that has been a staple of art world tittle-tattle ever since. This time, when Eluard returned to Paris, it was by himself. Gala showed up a month later with Dalí in tow, never to let the exuberant genius and gilt-edged meal ticket out of her sight.

In short order, Dalí figured out how to make the most of his eccentricities, first in France and then in the U.S. He was the first major Surrealist to arrive on these shores, washing up shortly before World War II, and his uproarious presence only reinforced the American notion of Surrealism as a moveable bedlam. The public was shocked, *shocked*, by the Spaniard's antics—such as crashing through the display window of Bonwit Teller in a bathtub, or dressing his wife up as the Lindbergh baby for a society ball at the height of the Bruno Hauptmann kidnapping trial—but it gamely came back for more. Although Dalí had already become persona non grata within Breton's movement by that time, for many Americans, even to this day, his cantilevered mustache and goggly eyes *are* the face of Surrealism.

Like many episodes in the Dalí saga, the above-noted *faits divers* have been hugely inflated by the painter's supreme gift for showmanship. Dalí freely revised and embellished his best stories over numerous interviews and autobiographies, a habit that spread the news even as it perversely assisted in its devaluation. For while Dalí's ability to self-mythologize helped make him one of the world's richest and most famous artists—second only, perhaps, to his compatriot and contemporary Picasso—it has also left his legacy somewhat in doubt, as the outrageous public persona threatens to eclipse his genuine accomplishments.

It was with such considerations in mind that the organizers of the 2004 Dalí retrospective at the Palazzo Grassi and the Philadelphia Museum of Art set out to rescue their man from the ravages of disrespect. "No other major 20th-century artist combines such widespread popular appeal with so much critical disdain from official institutions and historians of modern art," asserts Dawn Ades, the retrospective's co-curator and the primary author of its catalogue. "The current exhibition . . . intends to ask in what sense there is a 'real' Dalí behind the 'public masks' of the showman and the mythical identities he created for himself. One of our aims is to dispel generalizations and assumptions about Dalí's post-1939 work, long viewed as kitsch by artists, critics and curators."

A major reason for this disdain, Ades argues, is that Dalí "seemed deliberately to ignore the twin impulses of modernism: to express an individual self, on the one hand, or to pursue the medium for its own sake (which leads to abstraction) on the other." Instead, Dalí used his meticulously classical hyperrealism to stage "mental processes, psychical drives and other invisible forces that govern life," narrating a kind of collective psychopathology. Ably abetted by his impresario-wife (he and Gala married in 1934), Dalí repeatedly staged his inner demons front and center, turning them through sheer persistence into the ubiquitous Greek chorus of Western cultural weltschmerz.

He also gained a popularity that, by its very nature, helped alienate him from Surrealist orthodoxy and rendered him suspect in the eyes of posterity. In an age when artists made a badge of honor out of obfuscation and hermeticism, Dalí confounded expectations by creating images accessible to the highbrow, the society matron, and the average Joe alike—images that, as time went on, pandered unashamedly to the Church, Francoist Spain, and any other underwriter of his exorbitant lifestyle. The nickname Breton coined in 1939 for his former star, "Avida Dollars," was not just a clever anagram.

In keeping with its outsized subject, *Dalí* clocks in at more than six hundred pages and over seven pounds (but then, how many Dalí catalogues *don't* take up the entire coffee table?), presenting extensive discussions of some 250 works spanning his career, along with an encyclopedia of key people, places, and concepts in the Daliverse; a remarkably detailed and illustrated chronology (nearly one hundred pages' worth); and a selection of the painter's writings, from early critical articles to important theoretical statements such as "The Rotting Donkey" and "Conquest of the Irrational." The aim is clearly to impart as comprehensive a view as possible of Dalí as painter, draftsman, filmmaker, visionary, writer, and tastemaker, and in this the catalogue succeeds: one comes away flabbergasted at the wide reach of Dalí's magpie mind, the many influences he passed through and subsequently rejected, the media with which he experimented, and the fashions he indulged in (and sometimes launched).

Still, for all its merits, the book does not entirely add up to a satisfying reading experience. In part, as with the Ernst catalogue, this has to do with the academic writing style of the contributors—though a few, such as the underrepresented Paul Hammond and, in the main, Ades herself, produce refreshingly vivid prose. But it also has to do with the design of the volume: not only its heft, but also the fact that text and image are generally crammed onto the page (except when they leave room for excess white space), or that some of the major reproductions are garishly printed from apparently substandard digital scans. (I'll leave aside the surprising number of typos, danglers, inconsistencies, and factual errors.) Perhaps more than anything, by adopting an arch-traditional entry-picture format, the catalogue undermines its own crusade to get us to recognize Dalí as "one of the most original [voices] of the 20th century." Yes, the paintings are remarkable, particularly—and this despite the curators' stated aims—those of the 1930s. But here, duly surrounded by their comparative figures, alternate versions, and documentary photographs, not to mention the requisite two columns of sober commentary, they appear somewhat flattened, placeholders of an experience that happened elsewhere.

To be sure, no book, however fine its reproductions, can replace the experience of seeing an artwork in the flesh. (I'm reminded of an anecdote about the aesthete Norman Douglas, who, upon viewing Dalí's *William Tell* with its neon pink penis and rotting ass's head, ran out of the room blurting, "That picture will spoil my dinner. See you later. I must get some fresh air at once"—a wonderfully visceral bit of criticism that no facsimile could elicit.) But it can give us certain things that simple viewing cannot, by which I mean, in the best of cases, new insights into what makes a given artwork worthy of our attention in the first place. It can treat art as a story of living, breathing *people*, rather than of isolated objects. It can also use that artwork as part of an innovative design package that would make the book itself a thing of beauty.

Dalí, though it tries mightily, and with occasional success, to bring to life the dynamic inventions of its protagonist, all too often muffles them under a straitjacketed layout and standard-issue curatorial source-hunting, leaving one of the century's most flamboyantly articulate painters strangely mute. In the discussion of *Suburbs of the Paranoiac-Critical Town: Afternoon on the Outskirts of European History* (1936)—as the title suggests, one of the most absorbingly enigmatic of Dalí's works—we read, for instance:

> The central image of the artist's wife, Gala, invitingly holding forth a bunch of grapes, is framed on either side by a confusing array of incongruous objects, fragmented vistas, and eerie townscapes that reverberate with Dalí's personal history and his sense of place . . . The girl skipping rope that we see through the central archway is also a direct descendant of the child spinning the hoop in de Chirico's *Mystery and Melancholy of a Street* of 1914, while the swaying bell in the belfry behind the girl that functions as her "anthropomorphic echo" can be traced to an etching from the *Bizzarie di varie figure* cycle by the 17th-century Italian artist Giovanni Battista Bracelli.

All this is no doubt true, but what does it tell us that our eyes haven't already? Even if I hadn't spotted the rope-jumping girl's family resemblance to de Chirico, how much have I truly gained by having it pointed out to me (especially when that point is developed no further)? Not to put too fine a point on it myself, I learned far more from Dalí's pencil-and-ink study for the painting, reproduced on the following page, which shows how he conceived various details—Gala's cluster of grapes, the equine statue—as "paranoiac" transformations of the same object, than I did from this repertoire of curatorial associations.

Part of my dissatisfaction, I recognize, stems from the fact that many of the paintings under study don't seem to warrant the attentions being lavished on them. One of the unfortunate characteristics of Dalí's talent is that it is diluted by its own expansiveness, the moments of true genius crowded out by endless works of lesser quality. (My sense is that it was this squandering of talent, as much as the artist's unsavory allegiance to the political Right and his naked opportunism, that made Breton finally despair of Dalí, as he had earlier despaired of de Chirico for similar reasons.) Somehow, behind the dazzling glibness and provocative concepts thrown off like fireworks, the obsessive explorations and startling images—some of which are now part of the cultural lingua franca—I can't escape the feeling that there isn't nearly so much "there" there as we're being asked to believe. Some of these paintings are incontestably brilliant and stand the test of time, but too many others are facile or repetitious, ill served by the curators' insistence on treating each creation (especially the later ones) as a masterpiece.

In truth, there is something ironic or paradoxical about the wealth of commentary Dalí has inspired, because he is perhaps the Surrealist painter *least* in need of exegesis. Unlike Ernst, who concealed his emotions under layers of collage, frottage, and allegorical decalcomania, Dalí let it all hang out. Puzzling as they appear, his canvases make no bones about their psychic mainsprings, and are filled with images of paranoid delusion, fellatio, sodomy, and putrefaction, all latent content made manifest (a fact that bothered not only Breton but Freud himself). It is interesting in this regard to compare the two artists' visions of their mutual lover: whereas Gala in Ernst's murals from the early 1920s is blown up, transformed, unattainable, the Gala who appears in Dalí's many renderings is much more direct and present—mysteriously gesturing or with her back turned, perhaps, but always concrete. His portraits of her are both a celebration of his "sister soul" and an ongoing record of his neuroses, with little held in reserve. If we are to credit Ian Gibson's thesis in *The Shameful Life of Salvador Dalí* that shame was the primary motor of Dalí's life and art, it is nevertheless the most outspoken and exhibitionistic version of shame we are likely ever to see. Even later in life, when the Dalís were pursuing independent, and rather sordid, sex lives, Dalí publicly acknowledged his wife's infatuation with the much younger Jeff Fenholt (*Jesus Christ Superstar*'s superstar) by casting her paramour du jour as his model for a canvas aptly titled *Gala's Christ* (1978). Ultimately, Dalí doesn't need anyone to tell us how to view his canvases or to provide the keys to his obsessions. He'd rather do it himself.

2. My Aperitif with André

One of the factors that helped distort the American vision of Surrealism from the start was the relative paucity of its writings in English translation. What few texts were available during the Surrealists' wartime tenure in the Americas, in magazines like Charles Henri Ford's *View* and the Surrealist-dominated *VVV*, or in Breton's 1946 book of poems *Young Cherry Trees Secured Against Hares*, his first in this language, tended to be for initiates only. (It wasn't until the 1960s that substantial quantities of Surrealist writing saw the light of day in English, and only as of the late eighties has there been a serious excavation of the back-catalogue.) The fact that the renderings were often poor didn't improve matters, though this was not always the fault of the translator. The poet Edouard Roditi, who made a more than valiant effort to translate *Young Cherry Trees* while Breton was in New York, admitted feeling hobbled by having the author almost literally at his back: "Since he didn't know English, he'd show the translations to friends who didn't know much English either, and who would make suggestions I didn't agree with, but that Breton trusted." The results, not surprisingly, were to no one's liking.

It is a truism that the English and French languages don't work the same way, and Surrealist writing in particular derives many of its effects from its canny flouting of French linguistic bylaws. Its brand of surprise or humor is often based on setting up our expectations and then yanking out the proverbial rug. To take one example: the French language usually puts its modifiers after the noun, using the conjunctive prepositions *de* (of, from) or *à* (at, with, for), leading to such everyday constructions as *moulin à vent* (windmill, literally "mill for wind") or *brosse à dents* (toothbrush, or "brush for teeth"). It's not hard to imagine how the poetic mind at play might morph that *moulin à vent* into a *moulin à vache* (cowmill) or a *moulin à verbe* (wordmill); or how that *brosse à dents* could veer off into a *brosse à danse* (dancebrush) or a *brosse à danger* (dangerbrush). The problem, of course, is that in English you need to put the cow before the mill, and anticipate the surprise transformation before it's even a surprise. Otherwise put, the challenge lies in preserving the freshness, spontaneity, experimentation, humor, and excitement that characterize the best Surrealist poetry. Which is why so much Surrealist verse in English, whether translated or written directly, sounds stilted or phony, like an American with a mid-Atlantic accent or one who peppers their speech with Gallicisms.

Which brings us to the translation of culture, the most recalcitrant text of all. The fact that Surrealism was given a less than cordial welcome by the American mainstream is neither here nor there (after all, how welcome was it at home?); the real problem is that, even when it *was* welcomed on these shores, Surrealism remained a very precarious transplant. Generally speaking, Americans appreciate the humor of Surrealism, the puns, the melting watches and floating bowler hats, but less so the dark underpinnings of despair, let alone the political and cultural agendas. Dreams and the unconscious might be an exploratory tool for Breton and Co.; for us, they're more liable to be taken as a diverting parlor game. During their wartime exile in the U.S., many transplanted Surrealists found that the local terrain—lacking both the cafés in which to celebrate the daily rite and most of the preferred libations—simply didn't prove very hospitable; and even those Americans well-disposed to the movement found its rituals hard to take seriously. Julien Levy, who mounted some of the first exhibitions of Surrealist art in the States, describes in his *Memoir of an Art Gallery* (1977) one of Breton's attempts to conduct a Surrealist meeting soon after his arrival in New York: the more he tried to impose the kind of order that had naturally obtained at the Paris sessions, the more those present (including some who had previously attended the Paris meetings) broke into guffaws. In the context of this vast and confusing new world, the old rules of conduct seemed ludicrous.

As it happens, even in Paris the café culture of Surrealism was something of a translation, adapted from the decades-long practice of artistic cliques pursuing their debates over shots of absinthe, and most directly transmitted to Breton by the poet Guillaume Apollinaire. It was in fact

Apollinaire who catalyzed the Surrealist revolution—not only through the linguistic happenstance of having coined the word *surrealism* in 1917 (though in a very different sense from Breton's later use of it), and not only through his stature as café magus, which provided Breton (among others) with a ready model, but more than anything for having introduced Breton to another fledgling poet named Philippe Soupault. In 1919, Soupault, who would become one of Surrealism's founding members, collaborated with Breton on the movement's seminal text, the suite of automatic prose poems called *The Magnetic Fields.* That book later inspired Surrealism's more sustained experiments with automatism, and can fairly be considered the spark that lit the fuse.

Like Surrealism itself, Apollinaire was both a product of his surroundings and defiantly sui generis. Born Wilhelm Apollinaris de Kostrowitzky in Rome in 1880, he migrated to Paris at around the turn of the century and began engaging in the activities that have made his name virtually synonymous with the city's modernist explosion in the years before World War I. Apollinaire was a poet, essayist, novelist, art critic, chronicler, and man about town, a cultural omnivore and tireless promoter who championed Futurism, helped establish Cubism and Picasso, and seemed to have his finger in every fresh pie to come flying out of the French cultural ovens. His 1913 collection *Alcools* remains one of the foundational texts of modern poetry. Two years later, this elder statesman of the avant-garde met and befriended the teenaged Breton, sixteen years his junior, and encouraged his early attempts at verse. In his *Manifesto* of 1924, Breton, seeking to establish a pedigree for his newly formed band, drafted a now-famous list of forerunners, each one singled out as having been "Surrealist in" something or other ("Swift is Surrealist in malice. Sade is Surrealist in sadism," etc.). Apollinaire's conspicuous absence from this list—though he is granted somewhat backhanded homage in the preceding paragraphs—is not a mark of irrelevance, but rather a sign that he was too much of a father *not* to be discarded.

In 1911, Apollinaire had been implicated in the theft of the Mona Lisa from the Louvre, which left him with a brief experience of French prison (the charges were eventually dropped) and an abiding terror of deportation. When the war broke out, he enlisted in the French artillery, joined an officers' training program, and filed for naturalization. The poems he wrote from that point until his death just before Armistice Day 1918, collected posthumously in *Calligrammes*, attempt to salvage from the war experience a new poetic language, much as his earlier verse had celebrated such recent additions to the Paris skyline as the Eiffel Tower and biplanes. Apollinaire was the poet of perpetual wonder, finding his inspiration in the plethora of novelties that furnished the early twentieth century, from iron bridges to colloquial speech patterns to mortar shells bursting colorfully in air. His habit of infusing contemporary surroundings with a sense of classical harmony found its way into the modernist aesthetic and informs the poetry of Surrealism on down to the New York School: lines such as "31st August 1914 / I left Deauville a little before midnight / in Rouveyre's little car" ("The Little Car") would not be terribly out of place amid the chatty verse monologues of Frank O'Hara.

In *The Self-Dismembered Man: Selected Later Poems*, his second volume of Apollinaire translations,* Donald Revell is alert to the poet's drive toward novelty, and consequently chooses his English words with an eye to the entire nimbus of meanings surrounding them. This is one of the more laudable things about Revell's versions; the other is that he has selected from Apollinaire's expansive oeuvre only his favorite pieces—would that every translator should be so wise—and for

* Wesleyan University Press, 2004.

the most part avoided the calligrammes proper (a form that, Revell argues, translates with only moderate success).

A noted poet in his own right, Revell seems to approach these pieces less in a spirit of translation than of recreation from within (shades of Lowell's "imitations"). At times this leads to some felicitous phrasings, but it also entails some rather odd readings of the original, usually involving inserts of the translator's own devising. A case in point is the following passage from "The Hills," from which Revell draws the title of his book:

I am the self-dismembered man
Denatured detached
Capable of death incapable of sin

This is a striking image. The problem is, the accents of self-mutilation and mutation are, if not quite absent from the corresponding French lines, at least far less overt:

Je me suis enfin détaché
De toutes choses naturelles
[At last I've removed myself
From all things natural]

There are other instances, from the small to the not so small: street performers have "almost vanished" instead of migrating "to the provinces," a man "*au visage couvert d'ancêtres*" ("his face laden with ancestors") becomes a "crematorium-faced organ grinder," and fresh-cheeked girls near death are described in the translation, but not the original, as "tubercular" ("Cloud Phantom"). And then there's the poet's prescription for an aesthetic of "new sounds":

On veut des consonnes sans voyelles
Des consonnes qui pètent sourdement
        Imitez le son de la toupie
Laissez pétiller un son nasal et continu
[We want consonants sans vowels
Consonants that mutely pop
        Mimic the noise of the spinning top
A sustained nasal effervescent sound]

In Revell's version, this becomes:

I want only consonants no vowels
Consonants that fart insensibly
        Mimicking a small boy's spinning top
Sparkling nose-farts

("Victory")

With all due respect to Mr. Revell's intestinal functions, I suspect Apollinaire had in mind not so much a Bronx cheer as an aesthetic of sound that would capture the explosiveness of the fireworks constantly going off above his head: the verb *"péter"* applies just as commonly to detonations as it does to post-prandial gas.

But where Revell seems most often to come up short is in capturing Apollinaire's tone. These later poems in particular contain lines that became talismanic for the young Surrealists, and that Breton cited throughout his life. To take two examples:

Rivalise donc poète avec les étiquettes des parfumeurs

and

Perdre
Mais perdre vraiment
Pour laisser place á la trouvaille

These are rendered here as:

The poets compete with perfume labels

("The Musician of Saint-Merry")

and

To lose
Really to lose
To make room for the windfall

("Always")

In both cases, there is a flattened, expository tone substituted for the almost oracular injunction with which Apollinaire infuses these lines ("Compete then poet with the labels of perfume bottles"), which, to my ear at least, robs them of much of their magic.

At what point does a translation begin to slide so far from its source that it becomes something other? There is, of course, no simple answer. Often the proof is in the reading: one senses the poet inhabiting the translation or one doesn't. In *The Self-Dismembered Man*, Apollinaire's voice seems most often to crackle through a fog of interference, as if we were trying to pick up his signal on a battered wireless, with the interjections of his American translator breaking in and superimposing themselves like static. There is more personality to these versions than, for instance, to the blandly faithful ones by Anne Hyde Greet. I'm just not convinced that the personality always belongs to Apollinaire.

Sadly, drearily, a host of similar flaws awaits the reader of *The Voice of Robert Desnos: Selected Poems,* translated by William Kulik.* While Kulik's renditions of Desnos are less quirky than Revell's of Apollinaire, and more or less trustworthy as to the sense, they can be somewhat awkward, and certainly lack the fire of, say, Bill Zavatsky's

* Sheep Meadow Press, 2004.

passionate yet controlled renderings from several decades back. As with Revell, one has the feeling of reading the poet through a thick screen, one that filters out the nuance and, for lack of a better word, poetry, leaving only its facsimile. (To be clear, I am not one of those who believe that poetry is untranslatable. No less than with prose, there are versions that work and others that don't.)

Desnos is Surrealism's litmus test. One of the group's earliest adherents, he soon pulled to the head of the class with his star turns during the 1922 "sleeping fits" sessions described above. Breton, in "The Mediums Enter," singled out Desnos's remarkable utterances under hypnosis, and in a speech later that year called him "the knight who has ridden farthest of us all." The slumbers had actually been introduced to the group by another young writer, René Crevel, and at first it was he who came out with the most gruesome and fascinating tales while under hypnosis. Within days, however, Desnos was giving Crevel a run for his money. Photos of the period show him, heavy-lidded and with vaguely clownish face, reclining in a stupor, or else reeling off the fabulous spoonerisms that he claimed to receive telepathically from Marcel Duchamp, then in New York. His responses to questions while in a trance were considered oracular by those listening in:

> A. - The convolvulus and I know the hypotenuse. [. . .]
> Q. - Who is [Théodore] Fraenkel?
> A. - A gaping belly with an egg INSIDE . . .
> Q. - What will Breton do five years from now?
> A. - (*Drawing of a circle with its diameter*): Picabia Gulf Stream Picabia.
> Q. - Do you like Breton?
> A. - Yes (*the pencil lead breaks, then, legibly*): yes.

But Desnos had too fluent a talent for words and too great a taste for independence not to venture into areas Breton proscribed—such as journalism, music criticism, and later hosting a radio show in which he analyzed listeners' dreams—which eventually squandered the personal capital he'd managed to build. The ostensible last straw was his involvement in a bar named after Lautréamont's *Maldoror* (one of Surrealism's holy of holies, far too elevated to associate with something as lowbrow as a watering hole), which earned the former knight errant an especially vicious lancing in Breton's *Second Manifesto* and his expulsion from the group in 1929. Arrested during the Occupation for resistance activities, Desnos was deported to Buchenwald and died of typhus at Terezin in 1945, just as the camp was being liberated.

Desnos's selected poems demonstrate what a talented chameleon he could be. His early verses read like a compendium of favorite Surrealist tropes, their distinctiveness lying less in their originality than in the poet's ability to push these tropes beyond what any of the others were doing. He channels everyone: his fellow Surrealists, Duchamp, Apollinaire, and even popular songwriters (in the thirties, Desnos partly made a living from composing commercial jingles). Over the course of this selection, we see the histrionic automatism of the early twenties give way to exalted love lyrics inspired by Desnos's unrequited passion for the nightclub singer Yvonne George, then to the only slightly more settled stanzas for his wife, Lucie Badoud, nicknamed Youki, in which desperation yields to the sadness of getting what you've longed for and finding it's not quite what you'd imagined.

Many of these poems suggest a violent internal struggle between hope and resignation. These lines to Yvonne George, for example, no doubt the most famous Desnos ever wrote, wrest a sad triumph from the woman's very elusiveness:

I've dreamed of you so much you're losing your reality
Is there still time to reach that living body and kiss onto that mouth the birth of the voice so dear to me?
I've dreamed of you so much that my arms, accustomed to being crossed on my breast while hugging your shadow, would perhaps not bend to the shape of your body

("I've Dreamed of You So Much")

At other times, however, they display a vengefulness and paranoia that verge on the murderous. Desnos was a devotee of Louis Feuillade's *noir* serials, such as *Fantômas* and *Judex*, and his passions ran toward the dark and criminal. Breton once recounted how Desnos, during a sleep séance, chased Eluard around his own house with a steak knife and had to be restrained. One gets the impression that if Desnos hadn't had poetry for an outlet, he might have ended up a serial killer.

Desnos wasn't the only Surrealist mad about the movies. Many in the group, particularly during the silent era but also afterward, exalted such celluloid marvels as F. W. Murnau's 1922 masterwork *Nosferatu*, Chaplin's and Keaton's anarchic romps, and anything starring Musidora, the body-stockinged femme fatale who haunted several of Feuillade's feuilletons and a million adolescent wet dreams. But more than this, the Surrealists looked to cinema, particularly in its early, silent, supposedly unsophisticated days, as an emotional conduit more convincing and immediate than anything in literature or the plastic arts. *Nosferatu* offers an especially good example of how such films could fire the imagination. From the graininess of its deep shadows to the still haunting power of its special effects to its herky-jerky movements and spooky intertitles (Breton spoke of his particular "joy and terror" at one—not included in

English translations of the film—that read, "When he had crossed the bridge, the phantoms came to meet him"), it carries a charge that has not lessened in over a century, remaining far more potent in its low-tech ominousness than the slicker remakes by Werner Herzog and Robert Eggers: it's the creaky that makes the creepy.

Robert Short's *The Age of Gold: Surrealist Cinema*[*] provides an engaging and insightful, if sometimes flawed, discussion of what the Surrealists were seeking when they sat opposite a movie screen. "The Surrealists," says Short, "always thought of the cinema as a threat to the eye," by which he means both "eye" and "I" (clever fellow). Unlike the film critic Ado Kyrou, whose landmark thesis *Le Surréalisme au cinéma* claimed several dozen films as Surrealist in nature if not in allegiance, from *Fantômas* to *The Exterminating Angel*, Short and co-author Stephen Barber work from a much more limited playbook, narrowing the field to the Big Three: *Un Chien andalou* (1929) and *L'Age d'or* (1930) by Dalí and Buñuel, and Germaine Dulac's *La Coquille et le clergyman* (1928), based on a script by Antonin Artaud. However restrictive one might find this choice (though the book does make a reasonable case for it), *The Age of Gold* contributes a valuable recap of the movement's involvement with the Seventh Art, and the ways in which the two Dalí/Buñuel films in particular mirror Surrealism's philosophical and political concerns of the moment. Short also draws a crucial distinction between the qualities that the Surrealists were looking for when they *watched* movies and the difficulties they faced when trying to export those qualities into movies of their own—in other words, to reconcile their revolutionary enthusiasms with the Realpolitik of film production. As he notes, "The Surrealist mindset was inimical to the highly

---

* Creation Books, 2003.

un-spontaneous and disciplined craft habits that are required actually to get films made."

"Eschewing analysis," Short goes on, "[the Surrealists'] response to films initially took the form of verbal equivalents to the visual impressions a film had made on them or the emotions it had evoked." Breton once described this kind of emotional charge as "the feeling of a feathery wind brushing across my temples to produce a real shiver," which in the case of cinema might be triggered by as little as a few isolated frames or a single intertitle. He recounted how he and his wartime compatriot Jacques Vaché used to hop from theater to theater, stitching together a composite film far more potent than any individual one—a kind of synthetic criticism that no doubt said more about the Surrealist nature of cinema than any reasoned study. Short, unfortunately, prefers instead to stitch together quotes from academic sources, all too often relying on them to make his point rather than basing his critiques on direct readings of the films themselves. The result is an impoverishment of his otherwise rich discussion, which at times the author seems almost intentionally to tamp down; I can't help wishing that he'd brought to it some of the filmic excitement with which a book like *Ghost Ships* pursues its thesis. But such is the nature of scholarly discourse that, even when expecting a night at the movies, one can easily find oneself in a lecture hall, the screen's bright and magical rectangle reduced to a dim wedge of light at the podium.

3. In the Dark

Asked by an interviewer about his early years as a medical student, Breton hastened to point out that his "physical presence on the lecture-hall benches or at the laboratory tables should not imply a similar presence of mind." This remark pecked at my brain as I sat in a dusky amphitheater of the Sorbonne on a sweltering June day in 1996, spectator at and participant in a symposium marking the centennial of Breton's birth. As I listened to the umpteenth close textual reading of one of his poems or yet another exposition of his "hermeneutic devices," it occurred to me just how prescient René Daumal's warning had turned out to be. In 1930, Daumal, resisting Breton's attempt to co-opt his fledgling group Le Grand Jeu, had half-snidely, half-seriously cautioned the Grand High Surrealist against "one day figuring in literary textbooks." ("If we aspire to an honor," Daumal proclaimed, "it is to be inscribed for posterity in the history of cataclysms."). Six decades later, the textbook industry had absorbed Surrealism to a point I doubt even Daumal could have predicted, and today the trend continues unabated.

There are better ways to pass one's time in the dark. In his autobiographical narrative *Nadja*, for instance, Breton (who would have been horrified by the Sorbonne proceedings, or maybe just bored to distraction) wrote of afternoons spent in the Théâtre Moderne, where the actors "paid scant attention to their roles, barely listening to one another and busy making dates with the audience," and where "during the performance rats scurried over your feet" while you perched on a "staved-in chair." Sound awful? The benches of the Sorbonne might have been sturdier (if not more comfortable), but the flimsy, implausible spectacles onstage at the Moderne also left plenty of room for fantasy. Breton, inspired by one of the singers, dreamt of meeting a "beautiful naked woman" in the woods, and once saw an actual woman wandering nude among the aisles of a similarly squalid theater. Debatable sexual politics aside, how refreshing to view an auditorium in such black light! I can guarantee that nothing emitted by the succession of gray heads at the Sorbonne lectern was nearly so unexpected.

Normalizing events such as the 1996 Bretonfest are hardly new, of course. As far back as 1942, Breton himself delivered one of his major statements, "The Situation of Surrealism between the Two Wars," in no less ivy-coated a venue than Yale University. A decade later, the term "Surrealism" made its first appearance in the *Petit Larousse*, the dictionary of record for mainstream French education. Two months before Breton's death in 1966, the conference center in Cérisy, Normandy, hosted the first major colloquium on Surrealism—an event that Breton viewed with great skepticism.

He was right to be suspicious. By the 1950s, and despite protests to the contrary, Surrealism was widely considered a thing of the past. Breton's word for those who tried to bury the movement in the annals of history was "gravediggers," and it cropped up more and more frequently in his interviews during those years. Even as he continued to involve Surrealism in numerous political and aesthetic causes, maintaining that "the principle of its energy remained intact," overviews such as Maurice Nadeau's *History of Surrealism* (1945) only dug the hole deeper—and at least Nadeau's history has the benefit of telling the story with some brio. Its successors, in particular Gérard Durozoi's weightier-than-thou *History of the Surrealist Movement* (1997), stifle that story under so many minutiae that it's a wonder it has any wind left. "It is absolutely essential," Breton was already acknowledging in 1929, "to keep the public from *entering* if one wishes to avoid confusion . . . I ASK FOR THE PROFOUND, THE VERITABLE OCCULTATION OF SURREALISM." Is the well-meaning Durozoi the sort of "profane" interloper Breton had in mind when he wrote these words? No doubt he wouldn't recognize himself as such, and that might be a large part of the problem.

By now, college courses on Surrealism, theses and academic studies on Surrealist writing and art, lectures and conferences rummaging through its every aspect, are so commonplace that they barely register. Surrealist art exhibits, once a source of scandal, or at least intense novelty interest, have long since become an expected feature of the museum season. The gravediggers have entered the sanctum, and at this point no one even thinks to bar the gate.

Which is not to say that Surrealism must be excluded from the university or the museum. My first true experience of it occurred in those same Yale amphitheaters that Breton had visited thirty-five years earlier, and I'm grateful for it. But I was fortunate enough to hear of it from a teacher who could convey the brilliantly colorful human story behind the work, who brought it all to life with tales of Surrealists swinging from chandeliers at banquets or inducing hypnotic trances—the kind of juvenile, absurd, but nonetheless vital shenanigans that give such movements their salt, and their staying power. Catalogues such as the ones discussed earlier in this essay have their place, to be sure. My fear, however, is that many of the people who read them (or even, increasingly, who write them) are insufficiently familiar with the key texts of the movement, and that they will know of Surrealism only what previous critics or art historians have said. I fear that, more and more, our experience of Surrealism will be mediated by an ever-thickening corpus of scholarly commentary, which further obscures its spirit and removes us from direct confrontation with the challenges the movement continues to pose. And if that sounds like an exaggeration, consider that the notes to some essays in *Max Ernst: A Retrospective* refer exclusively to other catalogues, with nary a primary source in sight.

Naturally, we couldn't expect Surrealism to last forever, at least not in the same form. The centennial of its own birth is upon us, occasioning who knows what further hoopla at the Sorbonne. The movement had an excellent run, lasting a good half-century and, in some regards, getting itself inscribed in the "history of cataclysms," to use Daumal's phrase. It was also inevitable that it should wind up in the history textbooks. But to carve it up, dissect it, embalm it like any other artistic or literary artifact, is fundamentally to misrepresent what Surrealism was and is, yielding impressions as false as when we apply the term "surreal" to some humdrum coincidence or employ it as a synonym for "kooky."

In an early letter, anticipating the famous conclusion of *Nadja,* Breton voiced the credo that "criticism will be love or will not be at all." Ultimately, Surrealism's most significant contribution to cultural history might well lie not so much in its imagery (visual *or* verbal), iconic as some of this has become, as in its resolutely marvelous take on the critical faculties. This approach to criticism imbues the analytical discourse with a heady mix of personal reminiscence, flight of fancy, scattershot association, shrewd analogy, delirium, and intuition that demands to be experienced rather than described. It also underlies numerous Surrealist expressions, among them Dalí's "paranoia-critical" exegeses (used to most brilliant effect in his 1963 study *The Tragic Myth of Millet's Angelus*); Breton's famous pronouncement, "Everything leads us to believe that there exists a certain point of the mind at which life and death, the real and the imagined, past and future, the communicable and the incommunicable, high and low, cease to be perceived as contradictions"; and group surveys like the "irrational knowledge of the object" or the "irrational embellishment of the city." As forms of criticism go, such renegade attitudes and experiments are less static, less heavily *reasoned* than what we typically find in the kind of thickly annotated enterprise of which Surrealism is today so often the subject. However elusive and perpetually uncertain they might be, however resistant to definition and sober analysis, however dependent on a line of thinking that is (to use Breton's term) serpentine—or rather, because of all this—I believe they will lead us closer to a true understanding of what Surrealism had, and still has, to tell us.

Robert Storr, in his essay for the Max Ernst catalogue, includes a deceptively subversive caveat that should be heeded by any art historian about to embark on a critical article: "Not everything about Surrealism has aged well. Aspects of its method and rhetoric strike the contemporary reader or viewer as embarrassingly out-of-date, if not preposterous. Acknowledging this fact rather than evading or explaining it away is the necessary first step toward relocating and reconnecting with Surrealism's critical and imaginative essence."

To make such a statement in an exhibition catalogue is admirable, even if Storr's challenge is left largely unanswered by the writings surrounding it. The fact nonetheless remains, and bears repeating: any artistic or intellectual movement born of a vital impulse, whether Dada, Surrealism, Fluxus, or the Situationist International, draws its energy from a specific, unique amalgam of personalities, interests, talents, accidents, contexts, and historical realities. Any attempt to revisit and explicate that impulse after the fact can do no better than to "relocate and reconnect," or else risk draining the subject of its substance and its interest. There is no formula for this. It is much easier to recognize how it doesn't happen—by assimilating the movement and its participants into a smoothly contoured chronological flow, or by squaring off the messy, palpitating edges of the subject's life and work—than how it does. In the current state of art historical politics, ever tighter specialization becomes a stand-in for depth, and blockbuster exhibitions require big, fat, blockbuster catalogues. Meanwhile, our connection with the essence grows all the more tenuous.

As I noted earlier, Surrealism above all aimed, through a broad spectrum of means, to liberate and build upon the potential for marvels in everyday life. Heaven knows we could use a shot of the marvelous in these sad times, and a greater familiarity with Surrealism should be a positive thing. But with each new academic study or scholarly presentation, the principle of its energy fades further from view. The movement had its explosive phase, and its shrapnel has since been picked clean by legions of scholars; what we need now is to understand and appreciate it in a way that stems not from the head but from the heart and groin. If discussion of Surrealism persists, then let it be not only intelligent and informative, but also passionate, instinctive, and creative. Let it be based on a knowledge of the primary sources that is visceral as well as cerebral, and that can transmit the emotive and kinetic charge of the movement's best works. Or, failing that, let it not be at all.

PATABIOGRAPHICAL

Some years ago, as I was interviewing a cordial octogenarian for my biography of Surrealist panjandrum André Breton—often labeled, to his disgust, the movement's "Pope"—my interviewee suddenly leaned across the table and threatened me with "a sound thrashing" if I used the abhorred word *pope* in my book. I did include the term, of course, but not without trepidation—a fear that had little to do with the outrage of vengeful codgers and everything to do with disappointing those whose trust I'd spent years courting. It's a quandary for any biographer, particularly when writing about a figure who still inflames the passions of a fervent cult: Does one respect the insider's code and eschew those aspects of the subject deemed vulgar, indiscreet, or commonplace? Or does one acknowledge that, for the general reader, such inconvenient or well-rehearsed truths are an integral part of the story?

Alfred Jarry is something of a poster boy for literary cult figures. Like fellow turn-of-the-century French eccentrics Arthur Cravan, Raymond Roussel, and Jacques Vaché—though marginally more famous than any of them—Jarry has left a legacy based partly on an enigmatic, often hermetic, body of writing, and partly on an equally enigmatic, and more flamboyant, garland of anecdotes. Figures as diverse as Apollinaire, Picasso, the Surrealists, Italo Calvino, Philip K. Dick, J. G. Ballard, and even Sir Paul of Liverpool have acknowledged his influence—one that owed as much to Jarry's nonconformist attitude as it did to his writing. The literary historian Roger Shattuck enshrined Jarry as one of the four great French precursors to modernism (along with Apollinaire, Erik Satie, and Henri Rousseau) in his magisterial 1958 study, *The Banquet Years*; in France, Jarry's works fill three volumes of the Pléiade, the ultimate literary canonization.

The irony is that Jarry's eminent status rests mainly on the play *Ubu Roi*, an extended schoolboy farce, largely cribbed from former classmates, that reads like *Macbeth* rewritten by W. C. Fields and directed by the makers of *South Park*. The play, which premiered to a fabled uproar in December 1896, both secured Jarry's fame and sealed his fate at the age of twenty-three. As Alastair Brotchie points out in his absorbing but imperfect *Alfred Jarry* (the first full-length biography in English),* *Ubu Roi* also helped turn its young author from a literary aspirant into a curiosity, perhaps known more for the stories told about him than the ones he composed.

Alfred-Henri Jarry was born in Laval, France, in 1873, the child of a lackluster union between Caroline, a "whimsical, not to say erratic" mother, and Anselme, the indolent co-owner of a textile manufacturing business. When Alfred was almost six, Caroline deserted her husband and took their children to Brittany, the first of several relocations over the coming years. Brotchie maintains that young Alfred felt only "indifference" toward his father while retaining a lifelong affection for *maman*, but the dichotomy was perhaps not so clear-cut: Shattuck, for one, convincingly argues that Jarry, the "sensible maniac," inherited traits from both parents.

In his teens, Jarry was already displaying the irreverent wit, pugnacious humor, and colorfully crude language that would later make his rep. One schoolmate recalled that the puckish adolescent "delighted in attacks on our modesty. He loved to see our cheeks redden with shame and envy." The most notable of Jarry's targets was his physics teacher, a

---

* MIT Press, 2011.

pompous, reactionary incompetent named Félix-Frédéric Hébert, who for years had been the butt of his students' satires under the nicknames "Père Hébé" or "P.H." Well before Jarry transformed Père Hébé into Père Ubu, adding his own dashes of comic genius, the character's main attributes were firmly in place.

Jarry's Ubu, as Brotchie writes, is an "unrestrained and tempestuous being . . . bent only on pitiless self-gratification and revenge," "a personification of some of the less comforting aspects of the human condition." The bastard spawn of Rabelaisian excess, slapstick, schoolboy humor, and infantile regression, Ubu blusters and butchers his way through the play's five acts, dispatching both friend and foe "down the hatch" for "torture, twisting of the neck, extrusion of the nearoles, and disembraining," and despoiling his subjects with such neologistic weaponry as the "phynance-hook" and the "pschittasword." It has become a commonplace to see the rotund green Ubu—the fellow puts the *pot* back in *despot*—the epitome of self-serving villainy, with his cabal of sinister yes-men and his inclination to "destroy even the ruins," as an avatar for any number of real-life kleptocrats, including a certain orange president. But for all his repulsiveness, there is something undeniably seductive about Ubu's display of pure id, especially when expressed in such comically grotesque patois and delivered in an exaggeratedly precise, staccato monotone that became not only his signature, but Jarry's as well. Nor was it only Jarry who succumbed to his antihero's dubious attractions; before long, Ubu-speak became a fad.

The *Ubu* plays—as with any good franchise, the first one bore sequels—were not Jarry's only works. Brotchie calls Jarry a "writing machine," built of unequal parts classical culture, fanatical cycling, and devout alcohol abuse. The man who did everything to excess, including writing (and writing *about* excess), churned out a notable quantity of novels, plays, puppet shows, poems, adaptations, essays, theater criticism, and opinion pieces. He also penned the unclassifiable, posthumously published *Exploits and Opinions of Doctor Faustroll, Pataphysician*, Jarry's fullest exploration of what he termed "pataphysics," or the "science of imaginary solutions." But none of these works exerted the same influence as *Ubu Roi*, whether on Jarry's contemporaries, succeeding generations, or the author himself.

Stories abound of the shy, foppish young man adopting the over-the-top behavior of his obstreperous brainchild. One of the most famous anecdotes recounts how Jarry, who carried a loaded revolver, was shooting at champagne bottles on a neighbor's wall for target practice; when the neighbor rushed over to protest the threat to her children's safety, Jarry unflappably replied, "Should that occur, Ma-da-me, we shall be pleased to make you some more." Indeed, Jarry became so identified with Ubu that he became a virtual prisoner of his own creation: Brotchie tells of a luncheon hostess who, shocked by her celebrated guest's good manners, prodded him until he let loose with the expected vulgarities—not that he needed much prodding, such as when he loudly volunteered at a posh soiree that he "had the squits" (*that* hostess did not invite him back).

That such tales—and this biography contains many, often quite humorous—threaten to overwhelm the man behind them is no accident. Since adolescence, Jarry had been a master entertainer, able to charm or offend any audience. By creating his outsize alter ego, first onstage, then in life, and letting it gradually subsume his entire person, he made it possible to get away with virtually any self-indulgence. Even his friends, whose affections were often strained by Jarry's fecklessness and irresponsibility, could not escape the orbit of his persona. The magazine editor Alfred Vallette, who along with his wife, the novelist Rachilde, was perhaps Jarry's closest friend and greatest supporter, summed him up as "charming, insupportable, and delightful." Playing Ubu full-time was Jarry's ultimate defense against the codes of a world he didn't care to endorse, and it served him as well as anything until a surfeit of drink, squalid living, and poor health finally did him in at the age of thirty-four.

The consequence of such an all-consuming masquerade is that it is tricky to peel away the concealing layers. *Alfred Jarry* convincingly describes a man who orchestrated his own elusiveness, but for that very reason the portrait remains fragmentary and diffuse. To be fair, Brotchie is aware of the difficulties, and he occasionally breaks the fourth wall to tell us so: "The more settled Jarry became . . . the more disjointed his biography becomes." Adding to the self-referential quality of the volume, every second chapter steps outside chronology to concentrate on a theme—pataphysics, misogyny, the debate over Ubu's invention—thereby interrupting the narrative flow.

Alfred Jarry's attention to its own process is not surprising. Brotchie loves books (as founder of Atlas Press in London, he has published many authors influenced by Jarry), and reading his detailed descriptions of various early editions, one can sense his bibliophilic passion. He also punctuates his prose with enough nicely turned phrases to keep one reading, despite the occasional lapses into minutiae. But he is not a natural storyteller, and often can't pluck out the trenchant detail that reveals more than a paragraph could—the pithy encapsulation at which *The Banquet Years* excels.

There are a few criticisms one could level at this biography, such as its equivocal stance toward women (almost invariably portrayed as ninnies or shrews, apart from Rachilde), or its failure to illuminate Jarry's ambiguous love life. But its main flaw is its ambivalent tone, a swing between overdetailed exposition and colloquium-paper abstruseness. Perhaps Brotchie couldn't decide which audience to serve:

the scholars for whom the basic background and lively anecdotes are old hat, or the uninitiated for whom this book might act as an introduction to Jarry, amplifying and furthering the kind of revelation that *The Banquet Years* generated half a century ago.

Many biographers face this dilemma, but with Jarry it is even more pronounced. Few writers have woven published work and public persona into such a seamless carapace. And few are so in need of an intelligent, investigative probe into the life behind the scenes: Jarry at home, once the posturing stops and the absinthe high has worn off. *Alfred Jarry* provides many new facts, some pertinent analyses, and a clutch of outrageously amusing yarns. It's as good a biography as we're liable to get in English for some time. But it suffers from the same weakness as most portraits of Jarry, offering the usual chiaroscuro of insight and obscurity, never really seeming to, or allowing us to, know its subject—at least, no more than Jarry, stage manager of his own life and mythology, permitted.

LOVE IN VAIN

The legend is known to any blues fan: he was an eager kid sitting at the feet of his musical idols, borrowing the guitar he could scarcely play and generally making a nuisance of himself. Then one midnight he stood at a crossroads near Dockery's plantation, bartered his soul to the Devil, and was next seen coaxing sounds from his strings such as no one had ever heard before, sounds that won him the throne in the pantheon of blues deities.

It sounds like the stuff of a bad screenplay, but for decades a surprising number of listeners clung to this vision of Robert Johnson as a demon-powered freak. Recently, however, several revisionist histories have espoused the unpopular and less romantic view that Johnson was actually a dedicated and highly talented musician who wittingly produced masterful music. One of these histories, Elijah Wald's contentious but illuminating *Escaping the Delta: Robert Johnson and the Invention of the Blues*,* goes one further by claiming that Johnson's current place in blues history is wholly out of proportion with the importance he was granted by his peers. "As far as the evolution of black music goes," Wald writes, "Robert Johnson was an extremely minor figure, and very little that happened in the decades following his death would have been affected if he had never played a note."

For the latter-day blues cult, there is no denying that Johnson is considered the bluesman supreme, on a par with such pioneers as Armstrong, Parker, Dylan, and Hendrix in their own genres, and placed

---

* Amistad Press, 2004.

well above the musicians who enjoyed far greater influence and success in their day. Despite Johnson's scant and, at the time, largely unnoticed output (as far as is known, he recorded only twenty-nine sides plus twelve alternate takes, much of it unreleased in his lifetime), he now stands, in Greil Marcus's words, "as the most famous and influential blues musician who ever lived."

Johnson's long years of biographical obscurity have only heightened his mystique. Until recently, it was virtually impossible to separate the apocryphal from the actual. The man seemed permanently cloaked in seductive mystery. When the only two known photographs of him surfaced in the 1980s, they were greeted as a major revelation. (A much-contested third photo was later put into circulation.) The irony is that this obscurity is also something of a myth: despite all the questions surrounding Johnson, his shadowy life and equivocal death, more is now known about him than about practically any other bluesman of his era.

The most complete information to date comes from the meticulously researched biography by Bruce Conforth and Gayle Dean Wardlow, *Up Jumped the Devil: The Real Life of Robert Johnson.** They confirm, following others, that Robert Leroy Johnson was born in Hazelhurst, Mississippi, on or about May 8, 1911 (though some documents suggest birth dates ranging between 1907 and 1912), the illegitimate son of Julia Major Dodds and a farmhand named Noah Johnson. Julia had ten previous children by her first husband, Charles Dodds, and a few years after Robert's birth she left Noah and married a man named Will Willis, known as "Dusty." Charles Dodds, meanwhile, moved to Memphis with his ten children by Julia plus two from another woman, having

* Chicago Review Press, 2019.

changed his last name to Spencer to avoid being found after an attempted lynching. Robert Johnson himself was known variously as Robert Spencer, R. L. Spencer, Little Robert Dusty, or Robert Dodds—further obscuring the few official traces of him that remain.

Much of his childhood was spent living alternately with his mother and stepfather in Robinsonville, Mississippi, and with the Dodds-Spencer clan in Memphis. His schooling, already interrupted by his periodic changes of address, was further hampered by poor eyesight due to a small cataract in his left eye and—no doubt more so—by frequent bouts of truancy during which he played harmonica for his friends (though according to Conforth and Wardlow, his education was not nearly as spotty as previously supposed). It was most likely in Memphis that he first picked up some rudiments of guitar playing from an older brother and was exposed to the recordings of the early blues artists, notably Charley Patton. Patton was one of the most popular entertainers around, and Johnson, like many a young man then and since, must have identified the fashionable vogue of guitar blues as a way of escaping the farm labor to which he seemed fated.

By 1930, Johnson, then around nineteen and living with Julia and Will in Robinsonville, had married a sixteen-year-old girl named Virginia Travis, who died that year in childbirth—an event that some claim started his life of wandering, though in fact he remained in the area for roughly another two years. Soon after Virginia's death, he began seeing a young woman named Vergie Mae Smith, by whom he had a son in December 1931 (Johnson's only legal heir), and while Smith was still pregnant he married an older divorcée named Calletta Craft, whom he abandoned not long afterward.

It was also in 1930 that Johnson met one of his primary inspirations, the legendary bluesman Son House. Not only was House, by all accounts, a mesmerizing performer—in Elijah Wald's words, he "played like a man possessed by a fearsome and consuming spirit," and films made of him late in life tend to confirm this—but his success on the local dance circuit showed that one could indeed make a living with a guitar. Johnson was at the time grudgingly trying his hand at sharecropping, encouraged by his hardworking but narrow-minded stepfather, but on Saturday nights he would sneak out to hear House and his sideman Willie Brown (the "friend-boy Willie Brown" immortalized in Johnson's "Cross Road Blues"). As House would tell it many times in later years, whenever he and Brown took five, Johnson would pick up their guitars and try to entertain the audience in their stead, even though his unskilled playing threatened to empty the place.

It was House who contributed one of the earliest and most enduring pieces of the Robert Johnson legend, and a key component in the belief that he acquired his talent in a deal with the Devil. According to House, the young man disappeared for about six months, only to return with his own guitar and an exceptional ability to use it. This time, said House, "when that boy started playing, and when he got through, all our mouths were hanging open. All! He was gone!" Actually, most sources remember that Johnson was away from Robinsonville for several years, and that by the time House saw him again he was already an old hand at playing juke joints (small country stores turned into dance halls on the weekend), house parties, and street corners. Far from having gotten a quick fix of hoodoo magic, he had spent the time studying under a guitarist named Ike Zinnerman, putting considerable effort and drive into learning his craft. The starry-eyed wannabe had in fact made himself into a seasoned professional.

From this period on, Johnson would live the life of an itinerant musician, rarely staying in one place for more than a few days; as the song goes, hotfoot powder seemed forever sprinkled around his door. He traveled alone or with one or two other guitarists, some of whom have provided much of what is now known about him. Many remembered him as self-possessed, sure of his talent and ambition, and personable and attractive in public, though also moody, liable to disappear without notice. He was described as slight of stature but a commanding performer, with "sharp, slender fingers that fluttered like a trapped bird" when he played, in the words of his fellow musician and sometime road-buddy Johnny Shines. He was also fastidious about his appearance. "Robert could ride highways and things like that all day long," recalled Shines, "and you'd look down at yourself and you'd be as filthy as a pig and Robert'd be clean." One of the photographs of Johnson shows him in a natty suit and hat, legs crossed, guitar poised, smile brightly flashing. The man was an entertainer, and he knew that in the working-class venues where he appeared, elegance was in itself an attraction.

The evolution of the blues from the early big-band variety personified by Bessie Smith and Gertrude "Ma" Rainey into the more countrified (and male-dominated) sound of Blind Lemon Jefferson, Leroy Carr, and Charley Patton has been amply recounted. What bears repeating is just how much the country sound was developed by record companies seeking a new spin on the genre after the "blues queens" started declining in popularity. By the time Johnson began performing, this sound was already well established and had a familiar vocabulary of its own, composed of a ready pool of musical riffs and "floating verses" that traveled virtually unchanged from song to song and singer to singer. Rather than the raw moaning of primitive naïfs, in other words, country blues was mainstream pop music, like Dixieland jazz before it and hip-hop in its wake, made by savvy professionals who studied one another's records and followed the latest trends just as assiduously as modern bands listen to their competitors. And few were more adept at retaining and adapting what they heard than Robert Johnson.

The commonly held image of Johnson is of a desperately shy loner who avoided human contact and couldn't bear to face his audience. For many of my generation, this image largely stemmed from the Columbia LP re-issue of 1961, which provided both our initial taste of Johnson's music and producer Don Law's recollections in the liner notes of the terrified young guitarist at his first recording session, facing the corner in order to play—an image so striking that Columbia chose it as the cover illustration of a second compilation in 1970. Johnson probably did record facing the wall, but it might have had less to do with stage fright than with hiding his technique from the other artists waiting their turn to record, or perhaps with trying to improve his acoustics by "corner loading." By all reports, he seems to have had no trouble working the crowd at live venues.

On top of this, Johnson, like most of his contemporaries, had a far more extensive repertoire than surviving traces would suggest. Although recordings leave the impression that musicians such as House, Johnson, and Patton played all blues all the time, the reality was that, as traveling singers needing to draw a wide variety of listeners, they had to be conversant with the current hits and also with a mixed bag of jazz, country, and ethnic standards. "A performer whose entire recorded repertoire consists of blues," notes Wald, "might have been making his or her day-to-day money playing in a jazz group or a country hoedown band, or even plinking out Neapolitan mandolin melodies in Italian restaurants." We can hear this in some of Johnson's own oddities, such as the hillbilly swing number "Last Fair Deal Gone Down" and the up-tempo jive "They're Red Hot," the kind of humorous hokum that was common fare for crowd-pleasers like Tampa Red and the Harlem Hamfats. No doubt there were many other such oddities, which never made it onto wax for the simple reason that Johnson was being marketed as a blues singer.

One of the most riveting sections of Wald's book is his song-by-song discussion of Johnson's two recording sessions, which took place in a San Antonio hotel room in November 1936 and in Dallas in June 1937. What comes to the fore, apart from a fascinating dissection of how Johnson crafted (and sometimes re-crafted) his material, is how much he and the American Record Corporation were, in Wald's phrase, "going for some hits." Both the order of songs recorded and the company's choice of which cuts to release bespeak a conscious attempt to produce a commercially successful platter, one that would launch the career of a new and untried artist.

The first session yielded Johnson's only relative hit, the double-entendre-laden "Terraplane Blues" ("When I mash down your little starter / Then your spark will give me a fire"). Listening to the recordings bears out Wald's contention that Johnson before the mike was nothing if not a pro, fully in control of his arrangements. Some of his alternate takes are so similar to the originals as to be virtually identical, with every *whooo* and *hmmmm* falling at the exact same time. Others show him rendering the same song in different styles, perhaps as a reflection of how he retooled his own material in live performance, or possibly to see which version would appeal more to the record-buying public. "Phonograph Blues," for instance, was played first with the slow tempo and accompaniment of "Kindhearted Woman Blues," then immediately afterward with the up-tempo boogie arrangement of "I Believe I'll Dust My Broom."

But most striking of all, from a post-1960s perspective, is how little original material Johnson actually contributed to the blues idiom. Even leaving aside his covers of recognized standards such as "Walking Blues" and his obvious remakes of recent hits—"Sweet Home Chicago" reprises Kokomo Arnold's "Old Original Kokomo Blues"; "32-20 Blues" is so closely modeled on Skip James's "22-20 Blues" that at one point Johnson mistakenly lapses into James's lyric—we are left with a body of work that constantly draws upon and repeats itself: "Terraplane" resurfaces as "Stones in My Passway" and "Milkcow's Calf Blues"; "Ramblin' on My Mind" is a twin to "Dust My Broom"; "Kindhearted Woman", Johnson's most characteristic arrangement, returns as "Dead Shrimp Blues," "Little Queen of Spades," "Me and the Devil Blues," "Honeymoon Blues," and "Phonograph Blues"; and so on. With the exception of three or four truly unique pieces, it is not unfair to say that Johnson produced only about half a dozen songs in his career.

He was not alone in this, of course. Listening to the collected works of blues artists, whether Tampa Red, Blind Willie McTell, or Lightnin' Hopkins, is often an experience of déjà vu all over again. Personal style takes precedence over variety, and that's part of the charm. The riffs become signatures: anyone familiar with the music can tell after only a few bars a guitar break by Buddy Woods, or Mississippi Fred McDowell, or Elmore James. Moreover, these records were made to be released two songs at a time on a wax 78, not to be compared side by side on long-playing vinyl or CD. Yet the point remains that the more closely we examine the music, the more elusive are the features that set Johnson apart from his contemporaries. As Wald posits, Johnson's legacy might derive more from posthumous perception than from what he accomplished during his life.

That life was already close to an end by the time Johnson first entered the studio. He had spent the previous five years roaming the South and as far north as Chicago and Detroit, making the kind of modest but viable living that any traveling musician can recognize. He had traced for himself a career that was respectable but not remarkable. As Wald points out, even after his first recordings were released, they elicited more admiration for a local boy made good than recognition of a unique genius: "In Mississippi, Johnson's work was hardly greeted as revolutionary. His most celebrated talent, if we are to judge by the reports of his contemporaries, was his versatility, his ability to pick up new guitar parts as if by magic and to command a vast range of styles."

Wald prefaces these remarks by describing a class that he once taught, in which he played for his students a number of the great Delta figures who had preceded Johnson, and finally Johnson himself as the epitome of country blues. But instead of being duly impressed, the class "looked at me blankly. What was so special about this? . . . My students' reaction, far from being stupid or ill-informed, was closer to the reaction of most 1930s blues fans than mine was . . . Which is to say [they] were in the rare position of approaching Johnson by way of the records that preceded and surrounded him, rather than coming to him by traveling backward from The Rolling Stones via Chuck Berry and Muddy Waters—the path taken by virtually all modern listeners." These sentences contain the kernel of Wald's thesis, which is that Johnson, while indisputably "a unique and extraordinary artist," is heard these days through so many filters—musical, mythical, promotional—that we have all but lost sight of his true artistry.

⋆

The story of how this came to be is populated by well-meaning naïfs such as the aforementioned Don Law and the jazz collector and music producer John Hammond, both of whom helped to launch the myth of Robert Johnson as an untutored wunderkind; a host of later-generation enthusiasts such as Samuel Charters, Peter Guralnick, and Pete Welding; and on through the mainly British blues-rock guitarists of the 1960s. Hammond, as is well known, had thought to include Johnson in his landmark Carnegie Hall concert "From Spirituals to Swing" in December 1938, only to find that Johnson had died several months before. He instead played two of Johnson's records at the concert, thereby establishing a definition of the "Delta blues style" that, for white audiences, has remained virtually unchanged and unchallenged for nearly a century.

Indeed, by the time of his resurgence in the 1960s, Johnson's fan base had become almost exclusively white, while Black fans were listening either to more contemporary blues artists such as B.B. King, Bobby "Blue" Bland, and Etta James, or to newer currents such as soul and funk. The dichotomy, as Wald explains, simply extended a divide that had always existed:

> Black fans in the 1930s heard [in Johnson] a good singer and writer in the contemporary blues mainstream, with a solid beat, interesting lyrics, but little to distinguish him from a lot of similar and far-better-known stars. The few white fans who heard him at that time seem to have considered him a brilliant rural primitive. In the 1960s, mainstream black blues buyers who stumbled across an LP reissue of his work would have heard a guy who sounded like the old-fashioned countrified music their parents or grandparents might have liked. Meanwhile, young white fans were embracing the same recordings as the dark, mysterious, and fascinating roots of rock 'n' roll.

In other words, while a generation of white college kids, music critics, and rock musicians were rhapsodizing about Robert Johnson—and too often aping his playing and singing style in ways that call to mind Martin Mull's parody "Ukulele Blues"—the children of his original fans ignored him the way their white counterparts ignored Perry Como.

For Johnson fanatics of my generation, what turned us on even before we discovered the original versions were the reinterpretations that we all knew by heart: "Crossroads" by Cream, "Love in Vain" by The Rolling Stones (credited to the pseudonymous "Woody Payne," a record label invention), or "Traveling Riverside" by Led Zeppelin, not to mention the enticing glimpse of the Columbia re-issue on the cover of Bob Dylan's *Bringing It All Back Home*. Not only did Johnson's reputation precede him, but so did the reputations of our most hallowed rock heroes. It was Dylan who shrewdly observed (in Wald's paraphrase) that "the difference between the old blues singers and the young interpreters of the 1960s was that the young performers sang as if they were trying to get into the blues, while the older artists had been singing to get out of them." Wald takes this a step farther, suggesting that while Johnson was seen by his Black contemporaries mainly as a bridge out of rural poverty, for modern white audiences "he has been the dark king of a strange and haunting world, lost in the Mississippi mists and harried by demons—a legend more earthy, violent, and passionate than anything in our daily lives."

In his 1989 monograph *Searching for Robert Johnson*, Peter Guralnick speaks of the "apocalyptic effect" the music had on him and his friends, and points in particular to the terror produced by songs such as "Hellhound on My Trail." The song *is* in fact hair-raising, and stark, and thrilling, as few others in the blues idiom can claim to be. When Johnson sings in a voice of high-pitched desperation, with hard-bent strings weeping behind him, "I can tell the wind is risin' / The leaves tremblin' on the tree," who doesn't feel the loneliness and panic of someone standing alone in a storm at night, with no shelter and nowhere to go? In the country blues canon, I can think of only a handful of pieces—Skip James's "Devil Got My Woman," Memphis Minnie's "Crazy Cryin' Blues," Blind Willie Johnson's "Dark Was the Night, Cold Was the Ground"—that stand beside it. The song works because, whatever the specific context, it is an emotion we have all felt, and when we hear it, we really hear it. Eric Clapton and Keith Richards can find an outlet for that emotion by absorbing Johnson's music into their own; for writers like Guralnick and Welding, the outlet is words, and when trying to convey something so raw, it is difficult not to tip into hyperbole. Only an outsized legend seems big enough to carry it all, made larger with every retelling.

But what the legend hides is that many of these songs were, at bottom, less a cry *de profundis* than a plea for sympathy or, more to the point, a seduction attempt. Enormously attractive to women—one girlfriend called him "the cutest little brown thing you've ever seen in your life"—Johnson had a well-deserved reputation for his ability to score one-night stands, though perhaps not so much for the sex as for the meal and warm bed that went with it. "Women, to Robert, were like motel or hotel rooms," recalled Johnny Shines. "Heaven help him, he was not discriminating. Probably a bit like Christ, he loved them all. He preferred older women in their thirties over the younger ones, because the older ones would pay his way." This, too, is something of an exaggeration—Conforth and Wardlow, for instance, describe a much more committed relationship between Johnson and a woman in Helena, Arkansas, named Estella Coleman, mother of the future blues musician Robert Jr. Lockwood—but perhaps not all that much.

In its early heyday, blues music had a largely female audience, and Johnson's alternate emphasis in his lyrics on sexual braggadocio and self-commiseration shows that he knew his public. Compared with the sexual coerciveness of many blues lyrics—invitations to "go up the country" are almost always followed by the caveat that if the woman in question doesn't want to, someone else will—Johnson might have been less heavy-handed than his peers, preferring instead to offer invitations ("Come on in my kitchen / It's goin' to be rainin' outdoors"), or sexual enticements, or even decent human advice: "When you got a good friend . . . / Give her all your spare time, love and treat her right." The fact remains that many of his songs, too, were songs of seduction and manipulation. Even "Hellhound on My Trail," for all the genuine depth of its distress (or perhaps aided by it), contains the insinuating message that if only some "little sweet rider" among the crowd would take him in for the night and "keep his company," everything would be fine. It might please us today to think that this was a vain hope and no human love could cure the singer's soul-sickness, but no doubt it pleased Johnson more when the strategy worked, as apparently it often did.

And, finally, once too often. A central component of the Johnson legend concerns his mysterious death, variously attributed to poisoning, gunshot, stab wound, or syphilis, but almost always involving a woman. The most common version holds that Johnson was killed by the bartender of a small juke joint near Greenwood, Mississippi, where he was playing an extended gig. On Saturday, August 13, 1938, believing that Johnson was sleeping with his wife, the manager (or, in some versions, the wife herself) slipped him poisoned moonshine after one of his sets. According to David "Honeyboy" Edwards, who was traveling with him at the time:

> About one o'clock Robert taken sick when he was playing. All the people . . . was begging him to play, and he played sick. And they said he told the public, he said, "Well, I'm sick, y'all see, but I'm playing, but I'm still sick. I'm not able to play." And they said he played on and about two o'clock he got so sick they had to bring him back to town [about fifteen miles away].

Other accounts describe Johnson, driven mad by the poison, "crawling around the floor and barking like a dog." Johnson died the following Tuesday, August 16.

While some details still (and perhaps always will) remain uncertain, Conforth and Wardlow, in *Up Jumped the Devil*, have established what now appears to be the most likely sequence of events: that Johnson was indeed poisoned by the bartender at the juke joint, a plantation worker named R. D. "Ralph" Davis, whose wife, Beatrice, was having an affair with him at the time. Davis later confessed to giving the unsuspecting Beatrice a jar of corn liquor for Johnson, in which he'd dissolved naphthalin—not, he maintained, with the intention of killing him (naphthalin, a popular way of exacting revenge in those days, was rarely fatal), only of making him so ill that he'd pack up and leave town. But the poison exacerbated a previously diagnosed ulcer, leading to severe esophageal hemorrhaging, and Johnson died of massive blood loss, possibly combined with pneumonia, having spent the last three days of his life virtually alone in a back room, vomiting, coughing up blood, and in excruciating abdominal pain.

The death caused very little stir, most locals figuring that Johnson was just a wife-stealing dandy who got what he deserved. The folklorist and collector Robert "Mack" McCormick, who was writing his own book on Johnson (left unfinished at his death in 2015), cut to the heart of the matter when he termed the incident "a casual killing that no one took very seriously." The police did not investigate the murder, and no one, including Ralph Davis, was ever charged.*

---

* An edited version of McCormick's manuscript was finally published in 2023 as *Biography of a Phantom: A Robert Johnson Blues Odyssey*. Despite its title and the legend that had long surrounded it, it is not a complete biography of the musician, but rather a detailed record of McCormick's search for information about this endlessly elusive and mesmerizing figure—a kind of folkways *Quest for Corvo*. It

★

Both *Escaping the Delta* and *Up Jumped the Devil* contradict much of the received wisdom about the most honored figure in blues history with salubrious doses of common sense. Wald in particular, as a professional guitarist and music teacher, has spent many years absorbing not only the blues, but also the venues in which it is played and the life that surrounds it. He demonstrates an understanding and an objectivity about Johnson's songs, their relative share of originality and cliché, that lets them stand on their own merits, while clearing away much of the hocus-pocus that has been applied to them over the decades. Both books also offer the distinct pleasure of reading commentators who revel in their subject and treat it with palpable enjoyment.

That sense of enjoyment is what marks a major distinction between those volumes and *Robert Johnson: Lost and Found* by Barry Lee Pearson and Bill McCulloch.* Published mere months before Wald's book, it covers much of the same ground and cites many of the same sources, as if the authors had kept peering over each other's shoulders. At the same time, there is an evident difference in tone and purpose between the two. Where Wald is mainly interested in placing Johnson back in his

---

is no less fascinating for all that, and no less frustrating. Several years earlier, in 2020, Johnson's half-sister Annye C. Anderson published a memoir, *Brother Robert: Growing Up with Robert Johnson*, that gives a more kitchen-table view of Johnson as he was during his brief stays with family. While it contributes little that's new about Johnson the musician, it fills in precious information about his background and milieu—and, not insignificantly, contains yet another previously unknown photograph of him. It also relates in scathing detail the maneuverings over Johnson's legacy and copyrights, with a particularly damning portrait of historian Steve LaVere—one of several "white men who don't know us and think they own us"—who claimed (fraudulently, according to Anderson) possession of Johnson's publishing and image rights. The book is not terribly flattering to McCormick, either.

* University of Illinois Press, 2003.

original context, allowing us to see him as his contemporaries did, Pearson and McCulloch are out to indict the mythmakers and to debunk the legends that now surround him. And while Wald approaches his topic with the ease of a man certain of his beliefs (or, in some cases, comfortable with his uncertainties), Pearson and McCulloch frequently display the vehemence of proselytizers, almost an exasperation: like the Blues Brothers, they are on a mission from God.

Admittedly, there is cause for exasperation. The myth of Robert Johnson is thick-hided and seemingly impervious to contradictory evidence. It surfaces in such mainstream tripe as the film *Crossroads* (1986) and in the work of serious scholars such as Guralnick, who should know better, as well as in Alan Greenberg's screenplay *Love in Vain* from 1983, in which the taciturn Johnson comes off as a guitar-toting High Plains Drifter. It is also seen hovering behind Martin Scorsese's 2003 series of documentaries for PBS, modestly titled *Martin Scorsese Presents the Blues*. While the man clearly feels reverence for the music, you need only hear his description of Johnson as a "haunted prophet who must go into the desert to find his voice" to know which side of the story he is on.

Pearson and McCulloch examine a number of the commentaries on Johnson since his death, tracing the origin of each overblown bit of lore the better to deflate it, but they reserve the bulk of their prosecution for the Devil-at-the-crossroads fantasy. That legend did not originate with Johnson, of course: the huckster Legba and his demonic bargain are fixtures in African folklore, and similar pacts were ascribed to a number of accomplished musicians, from Peetie Wheatstraw, the "Devil's son-in-law," to Howlin' Wolf. In Johnson's case, however, it has become such common coin that even those not normally given to such fancy have been caught defending it. Guralnick, for instance, as paraphrased by Pearson and McCulloch, absurdly claims that "the soul-selling legend is the highest tribute that could possibly be paid to Johnson." Isn't it more of a tribute to recognize that the man had talent, and was able to convey that talent despite all the stones that poverty, hardship, and self-destructive behavior set in his passway?

The crossroads legend has fed on numerous pieces of "evidence," ranging from Son House's offhand innuendo about "Little Robert's" sudden mastery to Johnson's own song titles ("Hellhound," "Me and the Devil Blues"). Still, very little of this holds up to serious scrutiny, and Pearson and McCulloch's argument that "supernatural themes haunted not Johnson's music itself but *discussions* of Johnson's music" has resonance: one would have to be extremely invested in the story to keep believing in it after reading their book. But modern blues fans do like their brimstone, and many will no doubt find it hard to release Johnson from his Faustian bargain.

At one point, Pearson and McCulloch cite a question posed by the magazine editor Peter Lee: "Would we still be as mesmerized by [Johnson's] music," Lee wonders, "if there were no mystery surrounding his life?" Both they and Wald contend that, for many, the answer would be no. But it might be more accurate to say that many wouldn't have heard Johnson's records at all. Or, like Wald's students, they would have taken these records simply as part of the long blues tradition, and guiltlessly preferred the work of Memphis Minnie, or Sister Rosetta Tharp, or Leroy Carr, or Bukka White.

Still, there is something undeniably potent about Robert Johnson's music that cuts through the noise of decades and the static of hype. His records contain moments of near perfection that quietly reveal themselves after repeated listenings: the delicate solo in the first take of "Kindhearted Woman," the lilting slide break and murmured asides in "Come On in My Kitchen" (which apparently left both women and men in tears when he played it live), the sexy swagger of his middle eights. One truly gets a sense of this when listening to anthologies like the 1994 Smithsonian compilation *The Blues*, a 93-song overview that stretches from Blind Lemon Jefferson to Ray Charles. The set contains many memorable performances, but Johnson's stand out as few others can, commanding your attention and daring you to confuse him with his peers. Does it matter whether he bested his competitors by selling his soul or by working his long fingers to the bone? The point is: he bested them.

Myths are born for a reason. Well before the posthumous Grammy award and Hall of Fame induction, before CD reissues and the websites, there was something about Johnson's small body of work that set imaginations whirring. Researchers have ferreted out obscure town records and cloudy recollections; critics have added layer upon romantic layer to the legend, not because they sensed a good story but because the music forces one not to leave it alone, to do more than simply listen and appreciate. Something so emotionally stirring must have sprouted from unearthly roots, it seems to say. No one could have been that good without a boost from the beyond. In reality, no one *is* that good, and therein lies the sad danger: the more Johnson's music is hyped, the more difficult it becomes to appreciate its actual beauties.

Similarly, we resist the image of Johnson making music as a career, rather than from some dark compulsion. The idea of a man producing those sounds largely out of a desire to sell records seems unthinkable. His persona can accommodate every sin in the book—Satanism, womanizing, murder ("32-20 Blues"), pimping ("Little Queen of Spades"), alcoholism, fecklessness—except for one: venality. Likewise, our own sense of romance rebels at the idea of creative genius coexisting with a banal drive to carve out a living: surely there was more to it than *that*.

In this regard, perhaps the most honest comment on the Johnson legend comes not from the many pages written about it but from the small insert accompanying the 2011 *Robert Johnson: The Centennial Collection* 2-CD set, which advertises a specially crafted brew called "Hell Hound on My Ale." It is easy to dismiss this as base commercialism: many artists have made that particular pact with the Devil. In recent years, Johnson has become a similar industry through no doing of his own, to the enrichment of his purported copyright holders and the Sony Music Corporation. But there is no point in fantasizing that he was too pure or too haunted to indulge in such self-promotion. If Johnson had been given access to these marketing tactics during his lifetime, I have little doubt that he would have exploited them to the fullest. And his music would have been just as brilliant—no more, no less.

THROUGH A GLASS, AMOROUSLY

"It is much less a film than it is myself," Jean Cocteau wrote to a friend at the time he was making *Orpheus* (1950), "a kind of projection of the things that are important to me." As with many of Cocteau's programmatic statements, this one is both obvious—what filmmaker couldn't say the same?—and deceptively slippery. In his various artistic pursuits, Cocteau made no secret, nor spared the use, of things that were important to him, to the point where his personal obsessions (the snowball fight, the handsome bully, the talking statue) have taken on a whiff of the ridiculous. In this regard, *Orpheus* stands as one of the great exceptions in Cocteau's oeuvre, a *summa* in which he managed to take familiar ingredients, from the legend on which it is based to the auteur-director's well-rehearsed private mythologies (the poet, the mirror), and recombine them into something both unabashedly idiosyncratic and widely accessible. It is fitting that a work so preoccupied with mirrors and reflections should send back the image not only of its maker but, more than any of Cocteau's other films, of its viewer as well.

The Orpheus myth, as every schoolchild knows, speaks of a troubadour so gifted that he could charm men and beasts with his song. When Death steals his wife, Eurydice, Orpheus ventures into Hades to win her back. There, his artistry sways the netherworld denizens into releasing her, on one condition: Orpheus must not gaze on his beloved until they are back in the land of the living, on pain of losing her forever. Unable to resist, the poet looks behind him, Eurydice vanishes into the shadows, and the grief-stricken Orpheus is torn limb from limb by the Furies.

As with several other modern adaptations, most notably Marcel Camus's *Black Orpheus* (1959), Cocteau transplants the ancient poet into a contemporary setting without so much as a by-your-leave. Where he departs from other adaptations is in shifting the emotional center of the myth. In his telling, Eurydice is not so much the love of the poet's life and loins as (in her own estimation) a "very ordinary" domestic companion, fraternally cared for, sometimes barely tolerated. Played by Marie Déa, who had starred as the pure-hearted Anne in Marcel Carné's 1942 classic *Les visiteurs du soir* (another role in which guilelessness must contend with the supernatural), she is the cliché of the celebrity's wife, a figurine in a toy marriage.

The crux of the drama for Cocteau lies in the relationship between Orpheus and Death itself. Cocteau's ars poetica revolves around a dialectic of rot and renewal in which the poet must depart the mortal coil and pass into the "beyond" of true inspiration, then return to spread the word. As an artist who experimented with numerous forms and styles (novels, poems, plays, memoirs, drawings, paintings, films), Cocteau had undergone more than his share of these deaths and rebirths in an endless quest for creative transfiguration. In his career as a film director—notable mainly for the Orphic Trilogy of *The Blood of a Poet* (1930), *Orpheus* (his most acclaimed cinematic work, which took the International Film Critics Award at the 1950 Venice Film Festival), and its sequel, *Testament of Orpheus* (1959)—he often brought the theme of death and rebirth front and center; the whole of *The Blood of a Poet* was built on it. But whereas in the earlier work this theme was "played with one finger," as Cocteau wrote, in *Orpheus,* he "orchestrated" it. And not only orchestrated but gave it a distinctly erotic edge.

In *Orpheus,* Death is figured as an imperious woman, the Princess, played by the Spanish-born Maria Casarès. It is hard to imagine more apt casting. Fiercely emotive, intelligent, and politically committed, Casarès enjoyed a mystique stemming from her theatrical work during the war, as well as from her offstage involvement in the Resistance and her storied affair with Albert Camus. By 1949, when *Orpheus* was filmed, she had under her belt major roles in Carné's *The Children of Paradise* and Robert Bresson's *Les Dames du Bois de Boulogne* (both 1945). Her ability to project an alluring mix of severity and passion, to "burn like ice," as Orpheus emotes, is central to her command of the scene, and to our grasp of the poet's fatal attraction. As for Orpheus himself, Cocteau cast his onetime protégé and, it was widely known, ex-lover Jean Marais in the title role, having already directed him in *Beauty and the Beast* (1946), *L'Aigle à deux têtes,* and *Les Parents terribles* (both 1948) and scripted his lines in *L'Eternel retour* (Jean Delannoy, 1943). Charismatic, classically handsome, frequently high-strung, Marais was already something of a matinee idol. While his popularity might well have rested more on the strength of his Nordic good looks than on his acting chops, in *Orpheus,* his heightened, melodramatic style (his scenes with Eurydice are as drama-queeny as the highlighted pompadour he sports throughout) somehow jibes with the image of the poet that Cocteau is out to present: self-absorbed, oblivious to others, attuned to a reality that hovers above the daily mire of "baby clothes and bills."

The casting of the leads was more apposite than most viewers realized. Ten years younger than Déa, who was thirty-seven at the time, Casarès was well on her way to becoming, as one newspaper put it, "the most outstanding French tragic actress of her generation"; the fact that she was both an emotional rival on-screen and a professional one offscreen adds an extra shading of pathos to Eurydice's confused anguish. Marais, meanwhile, had recently been replaced in Cocteau's not so private life by Edouard Dermithe, who appears in the role of Jacques Cégeste (himself inspired by the poet Raymond Radiguet, whose premature death a quarter century earlier still haunted Cocteau). The upstaging of the waning idol Orpheus by the hot young Cégeste ("He's eighteen years old and adored by all") mirrors this extracurricular standing—most economically conveyed by the contemptuous snort the drunken Cégeste gives Orpheus shortly before Death's flunkies whisk him away.

Cocteau conceived of his films as poetry on celluloid, putting such traditional cinematic tools as plot and mise-en-scène in the service of a dense, absorbing overall atmosphere. *Orpheus* achieves this effect partly by combining unsettling avant-garde tropes with accessible imagery. Such motifs as the poetry-spouting car radio, the Princess's motorcycle henchmen, and the shabby grandeur of the Zone (the no-man's-land between life and death, shot in the ruins of the bombed-out Saint-Cyr military academy) at once derive from our everyday world and stand outside of it. And there are other touches throughout, disorienting but immediately legible: the negative landscape outside the window of Death's car; her black gown suddenly blazing white in her moments of fury; the mash-up of disparate Parisian sites when Orpheus chases her all over town (literally). "The closer you get to a mystery, the more important it is to be realistic," Cocteau wrote in 1950. "Radios in cars, coded messages, shortwave signals, and power cuts are all familiar to everybody and allow me to keep my feet on the ground." He also noted that Cégeste's cryptic radio messages were based on ciphered broadcasts from England during the Occupation (and admitted poaching the phrase "The bird sings with its fingers" from the poet Guillaume Apollinaire—a touch of plagiarism that neatly mirrors the accusation leveled against Orpheus by Cégeste's friends). Moreover, anyone who'd been subjected to a French Communist Party inquest—notably, the postwar purges of intellectuals deemed collaborationist, which Cocteau himself had narrowly avoided—could easily identify the obtuse judges and makeshift courtroom of the underworld tribunal; while Heurtebise's self-defense ("I was her aide") smacks, four short years after the fact, uncomfortably of Nuremberg. Pauline Kael once noted how Cocteau in this film "uses emblems and images" of recent European history "and merges them with other, more primitive images of fear."

Like poetry as well, the film expresses a number of personal conceits—the most resonant of these being the artist's despair over public incomprehension, evident in the contentious dynamic between Orpheus and the younger generation. A facile inventor with a keen desire for acceptance, Cocteau was the darling of the cautiously adventurous beau monde but the bane of the harder-core experimentalists—the Surrealists chief among them—who reviled him as an artistic fashion plate, a Jean-of-no-trades who aped whatever was trendy and had long since become yesterday's news. It doesn't take much imagination to substitute Cocteau's own conversations for the dialogue about relevance between Orpheus and a café doyen at the start of the film, or to hear echoes of his private fears when Orpheus complains that his "life had begun to pass its peak . . . stinking of success and of death." Nor is it surprising that Cocteau would identify with both Orpheus, the master enchanter, and that other great symbol of death and resurrection, Jesus Christ, one more oracle crucified by a vengeful, fickle audience. (Cocteau's first adaptation of *Orpheus,* a theater piece from 1926, had in fact begun as a play about Joseph and Mary, until he decided that "the inexplicable birth of poems would replace that of the Divine Child.") It may be pure coincidence that Jesus Christ, Jean Cocteau, and Jacques Cégeste all share a monogram, but it's an intriguing coincidence nevertheless.

As Cocteau wittingly or instinctively knew, there is a voluptuousness to martyrdom. The figure of Jesus *nailed* to the cross, the image of Orpheus being savaged by a horde of frenzied women, are not only powerful and enduring emotional symbols but also potent sexual motifs. Admittedly, in the film, Orpheus's death is much less spectacular than in the original story, more a street brawl gone wrong than an epic orgy of violence, but the encounters between the poet and his Death (his mirror, his twin) are unmistakably erotic.

Erotic and, at the same time, sweetly romantic, for at its heart *Orpheus* is a classic story of doomed passion. When, in the end, the Princess pays the price for returning Orpheus to the world of the living, the film reconnects with outsize tales of love and sacrifice, from *Tristan and Isolde* to *Romeo and Juliet* to *The Matrix*—not to mention the Western world's *ur*-myth, the story of Christ's self-abnegation so that humanity might be granted eternal life. "The Death of a poet must sacrifice itself to make him immortal," Cocteau intones in voiceover. Here, Death, in a final bid to save her beloved, willingly embraces the ultimate punishment, erasure even from the afterlife. The poet, meanwhile, awakes from the nightmare of his underworld quest into a fantasy of domestic bliss. This denouement is the least convincing and most blatantly artificial part of the film, for we know that Orpheus, for all his billings and cooings to Eurydice, is still in love with the Princess. Though the memory of this love might have been wiped clean, in the recesses of his creative unconscious he will continue, as he says, to speak of Death, sing of her.

Perhaps you have to be in love to truly make sense of this film; perhaps you have to be in that wondrous and all-too-fleeting suspension of emotional remove, when nothing is too corny and "no excess is absurd." When I first saw *Orpheus* as a teenager, in the wake of a dramatic separation, I immediately understood it as a film about unrequited longing, about love lost and henceforth unattainable. The sorrow of that parting abated long ago, but the sense of yearning remains in all its universality, ever and unexpectedly renewable. It is this aspect, which transcends gender and time, artistic fashion and self-conscious artifice, that preserves the freshness of *Orpheus* and its emotional impact. Without entirely knowing why, the poet will continue to sing of Death, to seek her out, until the day he goes to his own eternity—and even then he will not find her.

A CHILD'S GARDEN OF ECCENTRICITIES

Known, to some, as the Houdini of French literature, Raymond Roussel is also its Peter Pan. Though something of a specialty item, the consummate verbal prestidigitator—André Breton dubbed him "the greatest mesmerizer of modern times"—carried in his bag of tricks enough material for at least ten times his actual output, and devised the sort of technological novelties that invite comparison both with his idol Jules Verne and with another of the twentieth century's underrecognized oddballs, Nikola Tesla (underrecognized, that is, until Elon Musk sank his claws into the name). In terms of compositional mechanics, his celebrated *procédé* (method), though its full implications remain largely unexplored, has resurfaced in the writings of the Surrealists, the New Novelists, the Oulipo, and the New York School. But in many ways, Roussel was also the boy who never grew up. In page after page, readers of his books find themselves seated before a seemingly endless spectacle, staged, it would appear, for the author's sole benefit. And as with many children of privilege, which Roussel was in spades, any discomfort or damage suffered by the performer takes a distant backseat to the demanding tot's enjoyment.

Roussel's 1910 novel *Impressions of Africa*, with its titular whiff of exoticism and H. Rider Haggard derring-do, would seem tailor-made to appeal to a young boy's sense of thrill. On the Ides of March, somewhere at the dawn of the twentieth century, a boatload of European passengers bound for Argentina survive a shipwreck and wash up on the shores of the fictive African nation Ponukele. There they are taken captive by the vainglorious local potentate, Talou, and held for several months, until sufficient ransom can arrive from the home continent.

So far, we have the makings of a relatively standard adventure tale set in a far-off latitude where curious things can, and often do, occur. But these are no ordinary passengers, and this is no pastiche of *King Solomon's Mines* (though Roussel, a fan of popular fiction, might well have read the novel, judging by the similarity of the name Talou to that of Haggard's sovereign, Twala). In place of the intrepid Allan Quatermain, Roussel introduces a singularly gifted collection of castaways, ranging from circus artistes to inventors to scholars to theatrical prodigies, each, as luck would have it, a nonpareil in their specialty.

Indeed, very quickly the ostensible plot of African captivity falls away, yielding to the author's real interest: a series of minutely described performances given by these castaways, as part of a gala they have devised to while away the time until deliverance. Theater—or, more precisely, theatrical effect, the sense of marvel produced by magical and well-disguised artifice—proves to be the most formidable protagonist of *Impressions of Africa*, and the novel's various characters merely its instruments. The human plight of these characters, the suspense surrounding their release from bondage, ultimately takes on far less importance than the question of whether their performance will come off without a hitch—and even that suspense is muted, for the true motor here is not *whether* the gimmick will work, but rather *that* it works and *how* it works. One can easily imagine Roussel, an avid theatergoer in real life, gaping with juvenile glee at the kaleidoscopic succession of wonders he has devised for his own amusement, each one following the last in a seamless and flawless procession, forming a world that is itself (as one critic put it) "a theater in which people go to the theater."

The matter of performance is no idle conceit. Obsessed with fame, Roussel spent his adult life haunted by the alluring, and ultimately elusive, specter of public adulation. He described for his doctor, the renowned psychiatrist Pierre Janet, the sensation of glorious bliss he had experienced in 1896, at the age of nineteen, while writing his book-length novel in verse *La Doublure*:

> I was the equal of Dante and of Shakespeare, I was feeling what Victor Hugo had felt when he was seventy, what Napoleon had felt in 1811 and what Tannhäuser had felt while musing on Venusberg: I experienced *la gloire* . . . Whatever I wrote was surrounded by rays of light; I used to close the curtains, for I was afraid that the shining rays emanating from my pen might escape into the outside world through even the smallest chink; I wanted suddenly to throw back the screen and light up the world. To leave these papers lying about would have sent out rays of light as far as China, and the desperate crowd would have flung themselves upon my house.

Needless to say, when *La Doublure* was published the following year—at the author's expense, as its endless minute descriptions made it virtually unsalable, even for poetry—it occasioned no such desperate flings, and Roussel sank into a depression from which he never fully recovered. "Its lack of success shattered me," he wrote years later. "I felt as though I had plummeted to earth from the prodigious summits of glory."

He continued to write nevertheless, in an unceasing bid for public acclaim. First, he composed several more, equally hermetic, epics in verse; then, deciding that fiction was a surer road to bestsellerdom, the two novels that form his literary apex, *Impressions of Africa*—again published at his expense, as ultimately were all his works—and *Locus Solus* (1914). Finding the response to these books still lukewarm, Roussel set his sights on the theater as a more promising audience magnet. He hired playwrights to adapt his two novels for the stage, financing the productions with dogged persistence, spendthrift profligacy, and the obliviousness to ridicule of a Florence Foster Jenkins. But his preference for long, abstruse monologues over discernible action put the shows beyond the pale of audience tolerance, and they fizzled after only a few performances. Undaunted, Roussel then turned to composing original stage works, starting with *The Star on the Forehead* (1925)—its title a transparent metaphor for genius that figures in several of his writings—followed by *The Dust of Suns* in 1927. Like their predecessors, both were costly flops.

Roussel saw one last work into print in his lifetime, the book-length poem *New Impressions of Africa* (1932)—a work so demanding, with its myriad extended similes, lengthy footnotes, and multiple layers of embedded parenthetical clauses, that not even its author can have expected much success for it. After this, as Roussel's biographer Mark Ford notes, he "started to experiment with other possible means of recovering the euphoria of *la gloire*," including alcohol and barbiturates. He also traveled in grand style, despite the vast depletion of his fortune occasioned by his hefty publication and production bills.

In June 1933, Roussel and Charlotte Dufrène, his confidante, traveling companion, and "beard," checked into the Grande Albergo e delle Palme in Palermo, where he spent most of the day either cloistered in his rooms or being chauffeured randomly about the city; evenings were devoted to drug-induced transports. He suffered a first overdose two weeks after arriving, recovered, then was found in his bathroom two weeks after that, having clumsily opened his veins with a straight razor. This, too, he survived, and soon after he tried unsuccessfully to bribe both Dufrène and the hotel valet to kill him. Finally, on the evening of July 13, he swallowed a handful of barbiturates and went to bed, while the sky outside his hotel window exploded in an ecstasy of fireworks and people flooded the streets—the combined results of a local festival and Mussolinian pomp that, as Ford wrote, might well "have reminded him of the flames, the noise, and the turbulent crowds" of his dreams of glory.

Roussel died that night still seeking the solace of "a little posthumous recognition." In the decades following, his work was embraced by successive generations of avant-gardists, and he attained, if not the household-name status he so envied in the likes of Jules Verne and Victor Hugo, at least a solid reputation as one of the twentieth century's most original and influential *littérateurs*—a "writer's writer," to use the kiss-of-death phrase. Authors ranging from Edmond Rostand to André Gide, Alain Robbe-Grillet to John Ashbery, Italo Calvino to Georges Perec, Michel Leiris to Michel Foucault, have dipped into the source he revealed; Dalí and Giacometti took visual cues from his works, while Duchamp acknowledged that *Impressions of Africa* "was fundamentally responsible" for the *Large Glass*. Yet, as Robbe-Grillet and others have pointed out, there remains an inexhaustible core of mystery in Roussel's work, an opaqueness within its own transparency, that holds us at a spectator's safe distance even as it keeps our gazes riveted, our minds constantly worrying a puzzle we can barely conceive.

★

The Africa of Roussel's *Impressions* is not, to be sure, the Africa of geopolitical fact, but neither is it a pure product of the author's fancy. The late nineteenth and early twentieth centuries witnessed an acceleration of colonialist expansion throughout the so-called Dark Continent, and reports in the press and travelers' tales, alongside lurid imagery of popular adventure novels, helped foster the widespread European notion of Africa as that alien place where weird practices, unspeakable horrors, and unheard-of flora and fauna lurked at every bend in the jungle path. The backdrop of Roussel's Ponukele in fact contains many of the by-then-standard attributes available in most basic accounts from his day, including many cribbed from his beloved Jules Verne. As with the boulevard plays he adored, there is a stagy, conventional quality to the descriptions and sentiments that betrays the author's literary, rather than first-hand, experiences of the setting—and of life.

For all that, Roussel manages to avoid many of his day's most prevalent stereotypes about race. And while *Impressions* does contain such markers of casual bigotry as the frequent use of the word "Negro," or a certain bemusement at the Africans' demonstration of such "white" attributes as scientific curiosity, not to mention the requisite cannibals and human sacrifices, by and large both Ponukeleans and Europeans stand as fully fleshed characters, replete with the basic human virtues and failings—including a peculiarly Rousselian gung-ho adventurousness and willingness to oblige even the most outrageous requests "without having to be asked twice." As the original manuscripts tell us, this was both intentional and laboriously achieved. Over various revisions, Roussel progressively smoothed out what was initially a much coarser and caricatured portrayal into something approaching a kind of verisimilitude. (In Louise Montalescot, moreover, he creates a much more independent, capable, and exemplary female character than could be found in most "realist" fiction of the time.)

Roussel would boast that, although he had "traveled a great deal" (he listed "India, Australia, New Zealand, the Pacific archipelagos, China, Japan and America . . . Europe, Egypt and all of North Africa . . . Constantinople, Asia Minor, and Persia"), he "never took anything for [his] books" from these experiences. Rather than seeking to broaden his mind or discover new horizons, he often chose his destinations for their literary appeal: a trip to Tahiti, for instance, was determined by his admiration for the popular novelist Pierre Loti, who had set one of his best-known works there, while Baghdad was for him "the country of 1001 nights and Ali-Baba, which reminds me of [the operetta composer] Lecocq." The writer Michel Leiris, whose father was Roussel's financial adviser, later posited that "the outside world never broke through into the universe [Roussel] carried within him . . . In all the countries he visited, he saw only what he had put there in advance, elements which corresponded absolutely with the universe that was peculiar to him." Though Roussel had visited Egypt in 1906, and even kept a diary ("Went to see the Valley of the Kings—Cold lunch—sun—heat"), there is no indication that any of his cursory observations found their way into the book he would soon undertake: like Verne's Phileas Fogg, he had little interest in the surrounding countryside or populations. Later in life he took to voyaging in a specially built caravan (*roulotte*), a kind of proto-RV with only a few curtained windows behind which Roussel wrote in peace while the foreign landscapes paraded by unheeded. Photos of the vehicle suggest nothing so much as an outsized hearse.

Pierre Janet, in his 1926 study *De l'angoisse à l'extase*, which contains detailed notes on his sessions with Roussel (alias "Martial"), noted his patient's "very interesting conception of literary beauty. The work must contain nothing real, no observations on the world or the mind, nothing but completely imaginary combinations." Reading *Impressions of Africa*, one sees how far the author has drifted from the trade routes of reality in his descriptions of such "native" phenomena as moles that secrete an irresistible adhesive drool, or underwater sponges that spin like pinwheels under duress, or a giant zither-playing earthworm, or huge plants that (unlike their author) absorb and then project rigorously faithful images of their surroundings. Not to mention sci-fi inventions like a mechanical orchestra that runs on hot and cold fluids, grapes bred to contain entire miniature tableaux within their flesh, or metals so magnetic they could pull something halfway around the world. (As with many such inventions, what was once far-fetched eventually becomes commonplace: the automated loom to which Roussel lovingly devotes pages of explanation has been industry standard for some time; Louise Montalescot's "great experiment" sounds remarkably like the modern laser printer; and the battery-operated portable fan that Bex invents for young Fogar can now be bought for pocket change at the local hardware store. One wonders what Roussel would have made of such contemporary gewgaws as the iPad and streaming video.)

But the true originality of *Impressions of Africa*, as of most of Roussel's major works, lies not in its attempts to out-Verne Verne, but in an invention that its author kept scrupulously hidden from sight. For in virtually every case, the episodes, conceits, and details from which Roussel fashions his characters and their actions were determined not by authorial whimsy but by a highly regulated process in which language itself is the sole motor and guide. The genesis of *Impressions of Africa* lies in a short story written some ten years before, "Among the Blacks," in which the opening and closing sentences are virtually identical. Only one letter has changed in the passage from first to last, but on that small variant hangs the entire tale. As Roussel explained it:

> I chose two almost identical words . . . For example, *billard* [billiard table] and *pillard* [plunderer]. To these I added similar words capable of two different meanings, thus obtaining two almost identical phrases . . .
>
> 1. *Les lettres du blanc sur les bandes du vieux billard* . . . [The chalk-white letters on the cushions of the old billiard table]

2. *Les lettres du blanc sur les bandes du vieux pillard* . . . [The white man's letters about the hordes of the old plunderer]

In the first, "lettres" was taken in the sense of lettering, "blanc" in the sense of a cube of chalk, and "bandes" as in cushions.

In the second, "lettres" was taken in the sense of missives, "blanc" as in white man, and "bandes" as in hordes.

Once those two phrases were found, my aim was to write a story which could begin with the first and end with the latter.

In *Impressions of Africa*, the game expands to include not merely one altered sentence but a vast proliferation, in which moment after moment hinges on similarly complex invisible puns. The examples are numerous, but to lift the curtain on just a few:

The Luenn'chetuz, the ritual dance performed by Talou's wives that results in copious belching, was generated by a dual interpretation of the phrase *théorie à renvois*: both a treatise with annotations (*renvois*)—in this case, Talou's proclamation of his own sovereignty—and a procession (*théorie*) involving burps (*renvois*).

Revers à marguerite (lapel with a daisy in the buttonhole) becomes *revers* (military defeat) *à Marguerite* (the French name for Gretchen in Goethe's *Faust*), hence the rival king Yaour's downfall while wearing Gretchen's dress.

Toupie à coup de fouet (a spinning top set in motion by a yank of the string) leads to the episode in which the old frump (*toupie*) Olga Chervonenkov is paralyzed by a muscle spasm (*coup de fouet*) while attempting a pirouette.

The talking horse Romulus, a true platinum standard (*étalon à platine*) among equines, is also an *étalon* (stallion) *à platine* (with a tongue, in slang).

Maison à espagnolettes (house with window latches) yields the *maison* (as in dynasty) of the descendants of Suann, founded when the patriarch simultaneously married the two *Espagnolettes*, or young Spanish twins. (*Deux amours de Suann*? Given the frequent comparisons made between Roussel and Proust and the two men's acquaintanceship, we can only wonder.)

None of this was apparent to the book's few French readers, any more than it would be to their Anglophone counterparts today. Roussel the master magician kept his tricks well concealed, and stepped out from behind the curtain to tip his sleight of hand only in a posthumously published manual-cum-apologia pro vita sua titled *How I Wrote Certain of My Books*. With a mix of unvarnished literary altruism ("It seems to me that it is my duty to reveal this method, since I have the feeling that future writers may perhaps be able to exploit it fruitfully"), his lifelong hunger for recognition, and an almost infantile inability to withhold a really good secret, Roussel trots out example after example of his derivations like an especially clingy merchant intent on hawking his wares.

At the same time, the process by which Roussel gave away his creative method mirrors the dual movement already encoded in *Impressions of Africa*: first the magic, then the revelation of its workings. At the novel's halfway point, the author loops back to zero and starts his tale all over again, this time filling in the missing back stories and justifications for the many curiosities we've just witnessed. Some editions even included an insert suggesting that "those who are not initiated into the art of Mr. Raymond Roussel" might wish to read the second half first. This would of course miss the point, for the first rule of magic is to keep your audience tantalized: dazzle before denouement.

The novelist Harry Mathews once remarked that Roussel's language taught him how "writing could provide me with the means of so radically outwitting myself that I could bring my hidden experiences, my unadmitted self into view." Hiding, concealment, non-admission are sewn into the fabric of *Impressions of Africa*—not just the behind-the-curtain mechanics of Roussel's compositional generator, but likely something deeper as well: an incursion, despite himself, of the author's personal truth into the "complete illusion of reality" he sought to achieve. It's no secret today that Roussel's proclivities ran to younger working-class males, but during his lifetime—and for decades afterward—it was cause for scandal and blackmail, and a source of mortification to his conservative, socially prominent family. We should therefore not be surprised at the role that secrecy and subterfuge play in the various plotlines of *Impressions of Africa*, nor, perhaps, at the fact that no adult sexual relationship in the book ends happily, and that they often have the dispassionate tone of a business transaction.

Indeed, virtually the only true love to be found here is that involving children—either the kind of surrogate parent-child bond enjoyed by Velbar and Sirdah or, more often, between young quasi-siblings like Seil-kor and Nina or Meisdehl and Kalj. The painter and writer Trevor Winkfield notes that Roussel's own love for his sister "was one of the most formative influences of his life," and in that love seems to lie not only the kernel of the many idyllic brother-sister relationships in his work but an unhealed wound of nostalgia for the lost paradise of childhood itself. "Of my childhood I have preserved a delightful memory," he confided in *How I Wrote*. "I can claim to have known at that time many years of perfect bliss." So much so that he later said he'd felt no happiness since then, and that the memory of that former happiness was a source of torment. Just as Seil-kor, after Nina's untimely death, rejects the places they had loved together, so, according to Leiris, Roussel refused to set foot in "certain towns which evoked particularly happy memories of his childhood" for fear of spoiling them.

Instead, a spirit both childlike and childish infuses *Impressions of Africa*: marvelously, when it manifests as a constant openness to wonder, an ability to blur the lines of reality and fantasy without a grown-up's sense of restraint; naïvely, in its conception of a benign world in which the heroes all aim to please, and in which the cardinal danger is boredom; selfishly, when it treats the actors in the grand gala as mere tools of juvenile pleasure, taking it for granted that each performance will run smoothly and that nothing will break the spell; horrifyingly, when it indulges in the kind of pull-off-the-wings cruelty evidenced in the intricately contrived tortures and gruesome deaths of four convicts, a dark blood-spatter on the immaculate waves of Roussel's shifting, dazzling, treacherous, absorbing, blinding, engulfing African sands.

"LOVE AND THEFT": DYLAN'S APPROPRIATIONS

Poetry must be made by all. Not by one.

—Lautréamont

Anybody can be just like me, obviously.

—Bob Dylan, "Absolutely Sweet Marie"

. . . they're all *poets.* Y'understand?

—Bob Dylan, introducing his backing band, Royal Albert Hall, May 26, 1966

"You don't necessarily have to write to be a poet," Bob Dylan mused to a somewhat nonplussed Nora Ephron in 1966. "Some people work in gas stations and they're poets. I don't call myself a poet because I don't like the word. I'm a trapeze artist." With its mix of humor, incongruity, aggressive absurdity, and eccentric association, the statement is as good a self-encapsulation as any. It simultaneously incorporates and challenges treasured cultural artifacts: the link between writing and poetry, the "natural" blues of the workingman, the high-wire audacity of performance. It makes you nod at its verisimilitude, even as you want to go, *Wha?!?* For half a century, Dylan the trapeze artist has maintained a precarious balance between tantalizing us with his arresting composites and holding us at arm's length with his elusive burlesque. His ability to piece together a body of work and an identity, seemingly at the drop of a cowboy (or trainman's, or farmer's) hat, compels us to watch and listen even as he refuses to keep still, to gratify our expectations of what we'll see and hear.

Dylan's art has always been one of collage. His particular gift has been to appropriate, assimilate, and meld a wide-ranging mass of personal and national lore. The feeling of onrush that many of his songs can give, of freshness and daredevil collision, stems at least in part from the seemingly reckless nature of his juxtapositions—Ma Rainey and Beethoven, Beat 'tude and country corn, headline outrage and subterranean phantasmagoria, startling idiom and rank cliché. In his world, poetry has less to do with the best words in their best order than with an amalgam of street life and street smarts, aura and attitude, the language of composition and the language of cool; songwriting is less about expressing a yearning or inspiration than about preserving a diversified portfolio of loans from the cultural patrimony; identity is not an attribute you are born with or develop seamlessly over time, but something compiled from the flotsam and jetsam of accumulated experience. Nothing is static. Everything is up for grabs, reinvention, revisitation.

One can see this in Dylan's album liner notes, which dispense with the standard journalistic pap in favor of enticing glimpses of his thought patterns. One can see it especially in his interviews, which subvert the usual bid for favorable press coverage and instead become confrontational performance pieces—as in his cat-and-mouse fencing with *Time* reporter Horace Judson, captured in D. A. Pennebaker's 1967 chronicle *Dont Look Back* (Q: "Do you care about what you're saying?" A: "How could I answer that if you've got the nerve to ask me? Do you ask The Beatles that?"), or the petulant response he gave to virtually the same question at a Los Angeles press conference in December 1965 (Q: "Do you really feel the things that you write and sing?" A: "What is there to feel? Name me some thing . . ."), or his 1966 *Playboy* interview with Nat Hentoff, a masterpiece of comic surrealism (Dylan's oft-quoted answer to the question "Mistake or not, what made you decide to go the rock 'n' roll route?" begins: "Carelessness. I lost my one true love. I started drinking. The first thing I know, I'm in a card game. Then I'm in a crap game. I wake up in a pool hall. Then this big Mexican lady drags me off the table, takes me to Philadelphia . . .").

The critic John Hughes, in his book *Invisible Now: Bob Dylan in the 1960s*,* makes the point that these exchanges, for all their ad-libbing and wordplay, lift the normally banal rock interview into a realm of honest, if cryptic, communication between two people. When Hentoff asks Dylan "how he gets his kicks these days" and is told, "I hire people to look into my eyes, and then I have them kick me," it's not only a humorous slice of absurdity but also, Hughes remarks, "a fair enough account of his predicament"—at a time when the newly electrified Dylan was being booed, kicked by the very audiences who had paid to look into his eyes, and who presumably expected to peer into his soul as well.

"Surprise is our greatest new resource," Guillaume Apollinaire wrote in 1917. Surprise is jarring, uncomfortable, and rude; but it is also a bracing adventure. It was certainly an adventure for Dylan's early listeners. Used to hearing bromides about giving one's love a cherry with no stones, they were shaken out of complacency by songs such as "A Hard Rain's A-Gonna Fall," whose apocalyptic symbolism—part Child ballad, part Rimbaud's *Illuminations*—proved that folk lyricists could dig deeper into their bag of tricks, offer up more than just small change. Those who saw him perform live were in for even more of an adventure. The singer Dave Van Ronk recalled that Dylan "always seemed to be winging it, free-associating . . . He was a very kinetic

* Ashgate, 2013.

performer, he never stood still, and he had all these nervous mannerisms and gestures . . . He could put an audience in stitches without saying a word." It was a style of performance—since become a trope among those who have followed in Dylan's wake; and while he might not have invented it, he certainly helped legitimize it—that challenged the expectations of those come to see a politely ordered show, familiar renditions of familiar material. Nor was it aimed solely at the audience, for even Dylan's collaborators never knew quite what to expect. Joan Baez, in Martin Scorsese's documentary *No Direction Home* (2005), recalls what it was like to be onstage with Dylan in the early days: "He's gonna do what he's gonna do and he has to change and he has to keep moving and he has to add this and he has to crank the sound. And if you ever work with him, if he did the song the night before as a waltz, tonight he's gonna do it in two-four time just to fuck you up."

As a longtime listener, I never cease to be surprised by Dylan's facility at splicing in a broad variety of sound bites, from the sublime to the psychotic—among them the narrator's out-of-nowhere rejoinder about recapturing lost time in "Summer Days" (practically a word-for-word transcription of Jay Gatsby's incredulous remark to Nick Carraway, "Can't repeat the past? Why of course you can!") and the raucous marching-band intro to "Rainy Day Women #12 and 35," ripped straight from the 1966 novelty song "They're Coming to Take Me Away, Ha-Haaa!" by the one-hit wonder Napoleon XIV (not to mention from a million hometown parades). Most consistently, Dylan has used the rhythms, stances, and phrasings of the blues to give his songs shading and resonance, and even—itself a surprise, given the ubiquity of blues music—a certain freshness. Among the dozens of examples I could cite, there's the grinding shuffle "Pledging My Time" (*Blonde on Blonde*), in which he spruces up the tired indictment "He stole my baby" with the punch line "Then he wanted to steal me."

Though reticent on many topics, Dylan has never been shy about detailing the process underlying his compositions. "My songs are either based on old Protestant hymns or Carter Family songs or variations of the blues form," he allowed in a 2003 interview. "What happens is, I'll take a song I know and simply start playing it in my head . . . At a certain point, some words will change and I'll start writing a song." At the 2015 MusiCares Person of the Year Gala, he treated the audience to a lengthy peek behind the scenes:

> These songs didn't come out of thin air. I didn't just make them up out of whole cloth . . . There's nothing secret about it. You just do it subliminally and unconsciously, because that's all enough, and that's all you know. That was all that was dear to me. They were the only kinds of songs that made sense. "When you go down to Deep Ellum keep your money in your socks / Women on Deep Ellum put you on the rocks." Sing that song for a while and you just might come up with, "When you're lost in the rain in Juarez and it's Easter time too / And your gravity's down and negativity don't pull you through" . . . All these songs are connected. Don't be fooled. I just opened up a different door in a different kind of way.

Sean Wilentz, in *Bob Dylan in America** (a melting pot of older writings and new commentary), analyzes the process by which Dylan marries something borrowed to something old, new, and blue in the ballad "Nettie Moore" (*Modern Times*), loosely based on the 1850s lament "Gentle Nettie Moore." Dylan, he writes, "self-consciously reclaim[s]

---

* Anchor Books, 2011.

old songs and poems . . . giving them his own sounds and layers of meaning." Here's the first verse:

> Lost John sittin' on a railroad track
> Something's out of whack
> Blues this morning falling down like hail
> Gonna leave a greasy trail

And here's Wilentz's gloss:

> The first line is from "Long Gone Lost John," an old song recorded in 1928 . . . Dylan's third line, more familiar to American listeners, comes direct from Robert Johnson's blues masterpiece "Hell Hound on My Trail" . . . At first, it sounds as if Dylan means to sing an old folk song but can't get beyond the opening line: something's out of whack. But then Dylan appears to be playing a parlor game (or maybe a dressing-room game): give him a bit of old lyric, he'll think for a second . . . and then, boom, he comes up with a rhyming line of his own. "Track" and "out of whack"—why not? And why not take Robert Johnson's own rhyme from "Hell Hound"—"hail" and "trail"—but make the trail into something that's left behind and greasy.

Dylan's first avowed composition, "Song to Woody" (1961), was a blatant (and, given that it was intended to be played for its muse, rather brazen) rip-off of Guthrie's own "1913 Massacre." Several years later, he channeled his friendly one-upmanship with John Lennon into "Fourth Time Around," transposing Lennon's recent hit "Norwegian Wood"—one of the highlights of *Rubber Soul* (1965), an album directly influenced by The Beatles' meeting with Dylan, and retooled for its U.S. release to echo his "folk-rock" sound—into a more cynical key. Where Lennon's bemused suitor waxes wistful (albeit with an insinuation of spiteful pyromania at the end)—

I once had a girl,
Or should I say, she once had me
She showed me her room
Isn't it good Norwegian wood?
She asked me to stay and she told me to sit anywhere

—Dylan's, by being tougher and more venal, exposes the coy passive-aggressiveness of Lennon's courtship mores:

. . . And she worked on my face until breaking my eyes
Then said, "What else you got left?"
It was then that I got up to leave
But she said, "Don't forget,
Everybody must give something back
For something they get"

But it's not merely the situation that Dylan gleefully appropriates; it's the entire lyrical structure:

I sat on a rug,
Biding my time, drinking her wine
We talked until two
And then she said, "It's time for bed"

("Norwegian Wood")

I stood there and hummed
I tapped on her drum and asked her how come
And she buttoned her boot and straightened her suit
Then she said, "Don't get cute"

("Fourth Time Around")

Indeed, apart from a few minor variations in the chord changes, it could practically be the same song. Try singing the words of "Fourth Time Around" to the tune of "Norwegian Wood"—it works perfectly. More than just a repurposed love ballad, however, "Fourth Time Around" is a neat demonstration of artistic influence, in which Dylan uses this most Dylanesque of Beatles songs to chide Lennon for having borrowed from him in the first place: "I never asked for your crutch / Now don't ask for mine, *John*." The irony, of course, is that this is also a classic case of the pot accusing the kettle.*

If imitation is the sincerest form of flattery, then outright embezzlement might be seen as an act of deep devotion. "There isn't an inch of American song that [Dylan] cannot call his own," says Wilentz. "He steals what he loves and loves what he steals." Wilentz likens Dylan's patchwork approach to the American vernacular tradition of minstrelsy, which notably involves "copying other people's mannerisms

---

* Given the not-so-subtle dig, one understands Lennon's apparent schadenfreude in a well-known scene from *Eat the Document*, which Pennebaker filmed during Dylan's 1966 concert tour of Great Britain: sitting side by side in the back seat of a limo in the early morning, Lennon tosses off puns and bons mots while a hangover-green Dylan struggles to keep up, or at least keep his cookies. Nearly fifty years later, on the album *Tempest*, Dylan paid a sadder, less prickly tribute to his long-dead friend in "Roll On John" (its title taken from a New Lost City Ramblers song, as have been a number of Dylan's lyrics), which stitches together some of Lennon's titles and signature lines to tell his tale.

and melodies and lyrics and utterly transforming them." In so doing, he touches on an equally American tradition, the swift recourse to litigation, in which these artistic transformations are less charitably viewed as "a form of larceny." Suddenly, we find ourselves on the slippery slope that starts with cadging a line or two from an admired predecessor and ends up in the murky swamp of copyright infringement—and in that regard, around Dylan there's lately been high water everywhere.

Dylan's casual relationship with property is a matter of legend. In *No Direction Home*, several of his acquaintances from the early sixties lament the rare and cherished records that mysteriously vanished from their collections after Bobby crashed at their pads—a phenomenon that Dylan, in the same movie, sheepishly lays at the door of the "musical expeditionary" he then was. Nor was his piracy limited to physical vinyl: on his first two records alone, he looted his friend Dave Van Ronk's arrangement of "House of the Rising Sun" (thereby making it impossible for Van Ronk to record a piece he'd been honing for years); helped himself to a melody and several verses by another friend, Paul Clayton (himself a notorious copyright arrogator, according to Van Ronk), for "Don't Think Twice, It's Alright"; thinly disguised "Scarborough Fair" as "Girl from the North Country"; and appropriated the tune of the English ballad "Notamun Town" for "Masters of War." "If there's an original thought out there, I could use it right now," Dylan sings in "Brownsville Girl"—the operative word being *use*.

This isn't just a matter of filching a few lyrics or melody lines. Over the years, Dylan has affixed his name, after greater or lesser degrees of reworking, to a number of pieces that previously had been signed by others or consigned to the public domain, from "Lord Randall" ("A Hard Rain's A-Gonna Fall") to Elmore James's "It Hurts Me Too" to Muddy Waters's "Rollin' and Tumblin'." Suze Rotolo's memoir *A Freewheelin' Time* contains a humorous glimpse of Dylanesque cryptomnesia:

"Hey, you gotta listen to this song I just wrote! I just wrote it, or at least I think I wrote it, but maybe I heard it somewhere." As Dylan cagily told Steve Allen, when Allen asked whether he sang his own compositions or others', "They're all mine, now."

Dylan's supporters are generally willing to dismiss their man's pick-and-mix shopliftings as instances of the "folk process," whereby the unacknowledged borrowing of someone else's phrases, stanzas, even entire songs builds up a cache of materials that belong to everyone and no one, and that act as signposts rather than marks of authorship.

Since the loosey-goosey sixties, however, allegations of amicable pilfering have gradually hardened into stone-cold charges of plagiarism, and these have only multiplied in the age of Google. "Thanks to the increased sophistication of general-use search engines," writes Wilentz, "censorious sleuths could track down the tiniest pieces of Dylan's lyrics without having to spend months at the library." This scrutiny has revealed many uncredited borrowings in Dylan's work, including not only tunes ancient and modern but also, less comfortably, passages from Marcel Proust's *Within a Budding Grove*, which Dylan raided for his 2004 autobiography, *Chronicles: Volume One*, and the 1991 gangster memoir *Confessions of a Yakuza* by Junichi Saga, which makes several cameos on the 2001 album *"Love and Theft."* (The quotes were added to the record's title to show that it, too, was borrowed—from the historian Eric Lott's book on, appropriately, minstrelsy.) Some have reacted to this practice with the intensity of a lover scorned, seeing it, like so much else in the American grain, as a moral issue. Joni Mitchell, for one, lambasted Dylan as "a plagiarist" whose "name and voice are fake. Everything about Bob is a deception" (though she later claimed the remark had been taken out of context).

Jonathan Lethem offers a different slant in his 2007 article "The Ecstasy of Influence": literature, he writes, "has always been a crucible in which familiar themes are continually recast . . . The kernel, the soul—let us go further and say the substance, the bulk, the actual and valuable material of all human utterances—is plagiarism. For substantially all ideas are secondhand, consciously and unconsciously drawn from a million outside sources . . . Old and new make the warp and woof of every moment. There is no thread that is not a twist of these two strands." As Lethem freely allows, this statement is itself patched together from snippets—specifically of Twain, Emerson, and the German writer Michael Maar. William S. Burroughs wasn't aiming at anything very different when he observed, "All writing is in fact cut-ups, a collage of words read heard overheard." There is nothing new under the sun.

Adaptation, incorporation, and pastiche are among the favorite tricks of everyone from Picasso and Braque to Richard Prince, Sherrie Levine, and Shepard Fairey—though, as any newspaper will tell you, not always without legal consequences. In the words of Isidore Ducasse, the self-styled Comte de Lautréamont, who has become something of a patron saint of literary aggregators, "Plagiarism is necessary. Progress implies it. It closely grasps an author's sentence, uses his expressions, deletes a false idea, replaces it with the right one." Ducasse knew whereof he spoke: not only did he lard his book-length prose poem *Maldoror* (1869) with unacknowledged quotations from Romantic and picaresque literature, but he constructed his second and final book, *Poésies* (1870), largely out of retooled maxims by the great moralists—including the above-quoted one about plagiarism, which is virtually swiped from the eighteenth-century aphorist Vauvenargues. So is *Poésies* Ducasse's book, or should it more properly be considered the work of Vauvenargues, Pascal, and La Rochefoucauld? Similarly, if Dylan rewrites a few verses of "Rollin' and Tumblin'," is it still Muddy Waters's song or is it Dylan's? One traces with scant confidence the boundary between love and theft.

We might dismiss the matter as a topic for the old folks' home and the college, or for lawyers and music publishers; like many of Dylan's fans, we might simply turn a deaf ear. Not that the concept of property is necessarily meaningless. Yet the real judgment that posterity will pass on Dylan's work will have less to do with the verses and tunes he borrowed than with his process of assemblage—for as Max Ernst jauntily noted, "It's not the *colle* [glue] that makes the collage." Whether or not his songs will stand as works of art depends on how well he used his ingredients, on whether they do the job he asked of them. "A lot of [my songs] will last. A lot of them won't," Dylan told an interviewer in 2004. "They all came out of the folk music pantheon, and those songs have lasted. So if my songs were written correctly and eloquently, there's no reason they wouldn't last." Anyone can poach, but not many can do so while commanding the fascination of audiences for sixty years running. We can catalogue every bit and piece that Dylan purloined but we cannot quantify that.

"Bad poets borrow, good poets steal," T. S. Eliot is reputed to have said. (What he actually said, in an essay on the frequent borrower Philip Massinger, was, "Immature poets imitate; mature poets steal; bad poets deface what they take, and good poets make it into something better, or at least something different.") But the matter runs deeper than just a good poet stealing, and this is why I've dwelt on it here at such length. Call it plagiarism, appropriation, or the folk process, Dylan's approach points to an aesthetic future foreseen by Ducasse/Lautréamont, one in which "poetry must be made by all"—that is, by a multiplicity of voices, of selves, as against the Romantic notion of a singular genius. (The hip-hop technique of "sampling" is an obvious example.) Under the influence of the Internet and AI, creation is bound to become more hybrid and interdependent—and, I hope, better, or at least different, as well. "All my powers of expression and thoughts so sublime / Could never do you justice in reason or rhyme," Dylan confesses in "Mississippi" (*"Love and Theft"*). In order to say what needs to be said, maybe one needs to bring in a plurality of human expressions. Maybe it does take a village.

Still, I can't help wondering whether the outrage against Dylan has to do in part with the difficulty of reconciling his magpie approach with our cherished image of the artist as uniquely inspired. Perhaps we're offended because we're still in love with the illusion of the creator sui generis, who wrests material all their own from the depths of imagination. Dylan has always invited us to think of him that way, beginning with the tireless, impassioned rush of words in the "finger-pointing" years, and continuing with the oneiric, Rimbaldian flood of his "visionary" period. What so deranges our senses is the fact that Dylan, no less during those periods than in his recent work, called upon a process of composition that is acquisitive as much as it is generative.

The varied and sometimes intense reactions to this process form a key part of David Kinney's study *The Dylanologists** (the fact that such a word exists speaks volumes). Kinney's book profiles those at the far reaches of Dylanophilia: the ones who make pilgrimages to his haunts and homes; who attend "concerts by the dozens, and wait in lines all day [to] dash to the front of the stage"; who memorize biographical minutiae, "as if cataloguing these things will solve the mysteries of his life, and ours"; who—women as well as men—genuinely believe they are in a special relationship with Dylan and that "every song he writes he writes to them."

Extreme as these manifestations may be, they're not *so* far removed from the devotion inspired by other stars who achieved mythic status,

---

* Simon & Schuster, 2014.

such as Elvis or Sinatra. What makes Dylan different, possibly unique, is the minuteness of attention paid to his words, including those he borrowed—not so much to catch him out as to engage ever more meaningfully with the songs. Kinney devotes an entire chapter to listeners like Scott Warmuth, who has spent years teasing out sources for the lyrics on *"Love and Theft"*—everything from the Bible to Edgar Allan Poe and Edmund Spenser to obscure country and rockabilly tunes to a guidebook for New Orleans—and who finds the juxtapositions themselves a valid aesthetic act, additional layers to the message. Warmuth, he writes, "couldn't understand those who minimized the pursuit, as if appropriation was just Dylan's writing 'style' and there was little point in figuring out what came from where, and how it changed the meaning of the words." When it was revealed that Dylan had also leaned on previous writings to compose *Chronicles*, Warmuth dove into that book with equal zeal and admiration. "I think of it as the *Da Vinci Code* of rock 'n' roll," Kinney quotes him as saying.

But Kinney also discusses those who condemn any mention of Dylan's appropriations, "as if to even look for this stuff was tantamount to questioning the legend," and those for whom they are a source of disillusionment. The poet Roy Kelly, who had initially lauded *Chronicles*, was devastated to learn how much of the book came from outside sources. "'What did we praise him for then?' he says now. He felt misled, foolish, and let down—*personally* let down." As one longtime listener comments, "We invest so much in our Dylan experience that it takes on almost religious overtones."

Just as the appearance of the newly dandified, electrified Dylan at Newport in 1965 was a slap in the face of the folk faithful, so now the image of a Dylan cobbled together from others' words horrifies those who cling to the equally pietistic notion of absolute artistic originality. Religions, of whatever denomination, are powerfully addictive opiates.

★

All artists are amalgams of previous works, the sum total of the splinters lodged through a lifetime of being affected and afflicted by other people's offerings. Which is not to deny the epiphanous bursts that make artistic inspiration such a heady affair—the transitory brightness to which the mind in creation is awakened—or to denigrate those who experience them. At bottom, though, every phrase I've written here—every phrase written, period—as well as your reading of them, has been shaped, conditioned, or even dictated by millions of earlier phrases (such as the cop from Shelley just above), which themselves have been conditioned by, which in turn have been conditioned by, and so on. Even before committing a single note to tape, Dylan, like the itinerant street performers on whom he patterned much of his early public image, was a veritable jukebox of blues, folk, ballads, shanties, pop tunes, topical songs, and novelty ditties. Each of those genres was valued as part of the American musical heritage that has always informed his work.

No doubt the most encyclopedic expression of this heritage is the series of informal sessions recorded in an old pink house near Woodstock, New York, with members of what would soon become The Band in the summer and fall of 1967—that is, during the hiatus between Dylan's tumultuous 1966 tour and motorcycle crash, which put a full stop to his rock-star phase, and his reinvention as biblical sage with the gnomic parables of *John Wesley Harding* (released in late 1967). Mixing covers in various genres with finished and semi-finished original songs, the Basement Tapes, as they came to be known, owe a clear debt to Harry Smith's *Anthology of American Folk Music* (1952), the pond in which Dylan and virtually every other folk musician of his time went fishing, and into which Dylan has never stopped casting his line.

(In *The Old, Weird America*—originally titled *Invisible Republic*—Greil Marcus painstakingly tallies that debt.)

Though recorded as a lark, or as a way for Dylan to keep his hand in while deciding on a next direction home, the Basement Tapes are credited with inaugurating the strain known variously as Americana, alt-country, or roots music, and to a large extent with inventing the sound that dominated the next decade. (Or rather, since very little from the sessions circulated at the time, they exerted influence through their immediate offspring: Dylan's spare, laconic *John Wesley Harding* and The Band's grass-fed debut, *Music from Big Pink*.) In addition, the Basement Tapes, with their old-timey feel and repudiation of the "psychedelic shit" then fashionable—this was, after all, a mere two years before Woodstock became *Woodstock*—evince a contrarian spirit that is wholly typical of Dylan, and that says more about the American *non serviam* than any of his earlier "finger-pointing" material. "We were rebelling against rebellion," The Band's Robbie Robertson later quipped.

That included rebelling against their own rebellion, for among the things that the Basement Tapes box up and put on the shelf is Dylan's recent past. "We'd been playing blues and rock 'n' roll," commented The Band's Garth Hudson, "and all of a sudden here we were in a pink house in a beautiful place in beautiful hills . . . and that music wasn't suitable anymore." Sid Griffin, whose book *Million Dollar Bash** provides a who-what-when-where-how chronicle of the Basement Tapes, draws a distinction between the Dylan of 1967 and the previous year's embattled bandleader: "The spirit of the sessions was not one of us-against-the-world, as had been heard so loudly and proudly the year

* Jawbone Press, 2007.

before, but of friends . . . It was no longer music that pumped you up, it was music that invited you in."

What makes the Basement Tapes still worth hearing today is precisely this sense of open-endedness, the blind alleys and soulful, bounding leaps over a broad range of material—traditional ballads, contemporary pop, Dylan's own sketched-out verses—all of it filtered through performances that remove the songs from any identification with a fixed present. Jonathan Lethem has pointed out that Dylan's music, "while it famously urges us not to look back . . . also encodes a knowledge of past sources that might otherwise have little home in contemporary culture." In so doing, I would add, it urges that culture into a dialogue with the past that fosters its own evolution.

For Dylan, the privileged terrain of this dialogue is the romanticized West of the cowboy, familiar to generations of American kids. (In this regard, his early claims to have taken his pseudonym from the TV sheriff Matt Dillon, and his recent stage outfit—Stetson hat and suit with piping, halfway between Hank Williams and senior prom—are indicative.) Where *Blonde on Blonde* sought to capture "the sound of the street with the sunrays, the sun shining down at a particular time, on a particular type of building," this new music conjured up the frontier landscape of a thousand dusty movies.

That landscape has been portrayed many times, and perhaps never so evocatively as in Robert Altman's near-contemporaneous anti-Western *McCabe & Mrs. Miller* (1971), its bleakness underscored by an anachronistic but strangely apposite soundtrack by Leonard Cohen. What one takes away from the film, above all, is the sense of harsh incompletion, expressed in the relentless rain and mud and snow, so starkly different from John Ford's wide-open vistas; the muted tonalities that hark back to van Gogh's *The Potato Eaters*; the scaffolding that seems to prop everything up, as if the budding nation was already preparing to become one huge Hollywood backlot. We might also look to Dylan's appearance at around that time as the character Alias in Sam Peckinpah's *Pat Garrett and Billy the Kid* (1973), or to certain sequences in Todd Haynes's faux-biopic *I'm Not There* (2007), in which Richard Gere's Dylan-avatar wanders through a parallel-universe Reconstruction America, populated by a motley throng of carnivalesque figures with names like Tiny Montgomery, Mrs. Henry, and Quinn the Eskimo—the same figures who dominate the final reels of the Basement Tapes, at the moment when Dylan's songwriting seems to jump-start, to move past the cover versions he has been exploring and into new territory.

What is this territory? None other than Marcus's "old, weird America," or at least a convincing simulacrum; a fantasy, outlaw America, muted and sepia-toned, and yet somehow in perfect tune with the Day-Glo-weary, revolution-sick early seventies. Dylan's Basement Tapes composition "Don't Ya Tell Henry" imbues its rural tropes ("Now, I went down to the beanery at half past twelve / A-lookin' around just to see myself / I spotted a horse and a donkey, too / I looked for a cow and I saw me a few") with chugging blues-rock rhythms and a touch of postmodern detachment, nailing together several traditions like planks to build the path that much American popular music would soon follow. A little bit country, a little bit rock 'n' roll, this strain of music, typified by The Band (in songs like "Across the Great Divide" and "The Night They Drove Old Dixie Down") or Elton John's concept album *Tumbleweed Connection* (1970)—not to mention pablum like John Denver and the trio America—depicts a simpler land finding its way after the horrors of the Civil War. For the America of the late 1860s seemed not unlike the Vietnam-era America that, exactly a century later, was yearning for its latest conflict to end, and that could already smell on the wind the calamitous nature of that end. In times of great defeat, one often looks to a similar past that has already been survived. If acid rock captured the rage and hubris of the early Vietnam years, the Basement Tapes presaged a nation that had exhausted both.

But while the Basement Tapes might seem prescient today, it's important to note how resolutely out of sync these sessions (had they been heard) would have sounded next to the cutting-edge releases of that same year: *Sgt. Pepper's Lonely Hearts Club Band*, The Rolling Stones' *Their Satanic Majesties Request*, *The Doors*, Jefferson Airplane's *Surrealistic Pillow*, and Hendrix's *Are You Experienced*, to name just a few. The titles alone conjure up images of neon satins and harpsichords-à-gogo, whereas the Basement Tapes evoke nothing more glam than a bunch of dusty cowpokes and a tape recorder in a ramshackle cabin (which isn't far from the truth). In that basement, the sounds that would come to typify "Americana" were developed by a Midwestern refugee and a bunch of transplanted Canadians, who had deafened themselves to the ambient strains of psychedelia the better to attend to the rich, dark American substrata that the forgotten marginals on Harry Smith's anthology had cultivated, and from which their old, weird music had sprung. Only much later did it become clear that Dylan, while ostensibly delving backward, was actually steps ahead of the zeitgeist.

History repeats itself as farce. In June 1970, barely three years after the Basement Tapes, Dylan brought forth *Self Portrait*, a similar concatenation of old standards, new songs (some again sounding barely finished), covers of songs by his contemporaries (Paul Simon, Gordon Lightfoot), and, seemingly, whatever else struck his fancy. As he later admitted, "I just threw everything I could think of at the wall and whatever stuck, released it, and then went back and scooped up everything that didn't stick and released that, too."

One of the most reviled albums in Dylan's catalogue—Greil Marcus's review in *Rolling Stone* infamously begins, "What is this shit?"—*Self*

Portrait provoked as much hostile puzzlement as his "defection" to electric music five years earlier. It was one thing to give *Blonde on Blonde* and *John Wesley Harding* a bit of earthiness by recording them in Nashville; now, however, he had apparently bought into the whole country shtick, down to the syrupy strings, pedal steel guitars, and hokey album sleeve photos. Perhaps even worse, the idea of Dylan putting out a mix of other people's songs, when he epitomized the kind of singer-songwriter who made such mixes obsolete, affronted a generation that had come to look upon him as its very own Sybil. From the Every Mother's Nightmare of "One of Us Must Know" or "Obviously Five Believers" (*Blonde on Blonde*), he had morphed into a protective paterfamilias, replete with a "No Company Allowed" sign, a baseball bat behind the door to ward off his daughter's suitors, and a bunch of old numbers straight out of Mom and Dad's record cabinet. What is this shit, indeed!

While Marcus has gone down as the album's most virulent critic, he is by no means alone. The writer Clinton Heylin, a virtual Dylan industry unto himself, dismisses it as "outtakes and live oddities from one of the least interesting periods of Dylan's career," and potshots have been taken at it by nearly every Dylan commentator worth mentioning. Its unhip, white-bread tunes are bad enough, but what really seems to bug people is its underlying mood of contentment. "I once said I'd buy an album of Dylan breathing heavily," wrote Marcus in his review. "I still would. But not an album of Dylan breathing softly."

Farce repeats itself as history: not only did Dylan re-release *Self Portrait* in 2013, buttressed by copious outtakes and alternate versions, but the CD booklet notes were written by none other than Greil Marcus (who said Columbia Records has no sense of humor?)—the same Marcus who as late as 2010 had written, "What was painfully embarrassing then . . . is even more insulting now . . . What was mediocre then . . . is even more of a throwaway now," and who contents himself in the booklet with blandly praising some of the outtakes for their lack of overdubbed adornment.

Personally, I've always had a soft spot for *Self Portrait*. Some of the singing is undeniably schmaltzy, and some of the material, especially when compared (as it often is) with the compressed tension of *Highway 61 Revisited* or *Blonde on Blonde*, flirts with kitsch. But *Self Portrait* also has a loose-jointed charm, excellent musicianship, and a tongue-in-cheek knowledge of its own corniness that in itself is rather winning. In addition, the several songs presented in alternate versions ("Little Sadie" / "In Search of Little Sadie"; "Alberta" nos. 1 and 2) offered an early peek into Dylan's experiments with performance styles, at a time when such peeks were much rarer than they are now.

One reason I like the album, I admit, is that it came out just as I was discovering Dylan. Being younger than writers like Marcus and Wilentz, I didn't experience the headiness of first hearing *Bringing It All Back Home* or *Blonde on Blonde* in their original context. By the time I heard them, they had already begun slipping into history, while the Dylan I first met was celebrating the new morning and watching the river flow. In other words, I was able to take *Self Portrait* on its own terms, as an eclectic suite of tunes rather than an insult. More to the point, the album, at least in hindsight, seems very much like a continuation of the Basement Tapes by other means: it, too, tries to piece together a musical and cultural identity from accumulated musical traces. Were one to strip away its Nashville studio sound and Bob Johnston-style production and replace them with home-recording rawness, much of *Self Portrait* would sound remarkably like the Basement Tapes. (That the tight relation between the two was not lost on Dylan is suggested by his having followed the reissue of *Self Portrait*, in the Bootleg Series, with the first official release of the complete Basement Tapes sessions.) Looked at another way, what Dylan is doing with

Self Portrait is hardly different from what he had already done on his first album or in his covers of songs from Smith's *Anthology*, and would later do more overtly on *Good As I Been to You* and *World Gone Wrong*, and later still in his explorations of the Great American Songbook: recharging his batteries by plugging into the vernacular traditions that have always informed his music and our common culture.

Ultimately, though, what I find most interesting about *Self Portrait* is the statement it makes about artistic integrity, in its twin senses of "honesty" and "consistency." It's not just that the album contains such different material from Dylan's previous compilations—you could say as much of many of his records—or that it's such a disparate selection. Rather, it's that he changes so radically from track to track, as if each gap between songs were a false door through which he disappeared and reappeared in another guise. There seems to be little discernible relationship between the Dylan who warbles "Blue Moon" (a twist on the country lilt of *Nashville Skyline*), the one who rasps "It Hurts Me Too," the one who barks "Days of 49," and the one who yawps a live version of "Like a Rolling Stone" ("enough to make your speakers wilt," wrote Marcus, not meaning it kindly). Physically, emotionally, politically, philosophically, and artistically, the voice seems to emanate from someone else every time.

While *Self Portrait* raised eyebrows and hackles by marking a blatant about-face from the inner-dredged visions of *Blonde on Blonde*, what it really turns away from is the sense of a coherent performing (or writing) entity. Dylan's music has always contained a heteroclite blend of other people's songs and attitudes, but much of that was lost in the proverbial shuffle. *Self Portrait*, like the Basement Tapes, takes this process and gives us an exploded view of it, a glimpse into the laboratory. Marcus seems to have missed this point in his review: "It's certainly an odd self portrait . . . If the title is serious, Dylan no longer cares about making music and would just as soon define himself on someone else's terms." But isn't that what Dylan has always done—define himself, if not on someone else's terms, then at least via someone else's music? Doesn't that composite portrait go to the heart of who "Bob Dylan" has been from the start? And couldn't the same be said, to a greater or lesser extent, of us all?

To push the matter, we might consider that the self-portrait is also a mirror, a portrait of Dylan's listeners—or else a test of their ability to keep pace as he tries on new aspects like so many hats. (That he knew many would fail this test was made clear by his characterization of the album as "something [the fans] can't possibly like, they can't relate to.") The music writer Paul Williams once reflected that the bond between Dylan's avid followers and his music is "so intense [that] more than once over the years they've turned really nasty when he chose to deliver something other than their notion of who 'Bob Dylan' should be." In this regard, Dylan's piecing together of a writing or performing persona from fragments of others' words and deeds ultimately reflects the process by which we, his ever-changing audience, have been receiving his art since the beginning: fashioning our own Dylans, in our own image, even as he incarnates the images he chooses of himself. The point that he seems to be bringing home here is that identity—his, ours, identity *tout court*, especially in this invisible republic of reinvented lives—is, like his much-decried album, a matter of what sticks to the wall.

★

"I don't think of myself as Bob Dylan," Dylan wrote in the liner notes to his 1985 compilation *Biograph*. "It's like Rimbaud said, 'I is another.'" In fact, Dylan has been playing with the otherness of identity—its shifting, fragmentary nature, its illusions and deceits, its "continual state of becoming," as he later said—at least since he adopted the teenage stage name Elston Gunn. Whether it's Bob Dylan, Alias, Jack Frost, Jack Fate, Elmer Johnson, Tedham Porterhouse, Robert Milkwood Thomas, Blind Boy Grunt, or any other name that Robert Allen Zimmerman has used to identify and conceal himself, donning bits and pieces of other identities is a way of both creating and shedding a skin, of remaining at once present and, as the film title put it, masked and anonymous, hidden in plain sight. Dylan's art is one of reinvention: of himself, of his material, of others' material. And the leaps he makes from album to album, the changes in personal and musical style, the reworkings of bits and bobs gathered from myriad sources, are what have kept the music alive for so many decades, what "make it new," as Pound said. In those leaps, and the void under them, his imagination flourishes.

In his biography *Who Is That Man?*,* David Dalton notes that the narrator in Dylan's songs "is as much a character as any of the people in it." Similarly, he likens Dylan's mid-1960s record covers to "stills from his inner ongoing movie cycle." Think of the difference between the neophyte folkie of his 1962 debut, all trainman's hat and puppy fat, and the lean, petulant proto-punk of 1965. In fact, not only these covers but virtually all his studio album photos (at least through *"Love and Theft"*) are like stills from a film that is by turns gritty, surreal, noir, romantic, adventurous, and animated; they almost seem part of his own private Cindy Sherman installation, or a flipbook of himself aging.

But while each of these portraits constitutes as much of a performance as the music inside, each is also true to the Dylan singing that

---

* Hyperion, 2012.

particular group of songs. At his historic concert at Philharmonic Hall in October 1964, he quipped to the audience, "It's just Halloween. I've got my Bob Dylan mask on"—sneaking through the stage door of humor the sober truth that the figure his listeners considered "theirs" was in large part another bit of face paint. The real joke is that Dylan himself, at least for a while, seems to have believed in the mask, and he became furious whenever someone tried to remove it—as when his artfully concealed family name and background were outed in a 1963 *Newsweek* profile. Yet telling lies about oneself was hardly original to Dylan, and practically de rigueur in the Greenwich Village folk scene. "It was an old showbiz tradition—everybody changed their names and invented stories about themselves," Dave Van Ronk remarks. "So we kidded [Dylan] some, but nobody held it against him. I don't think Bobby ever understood that. He never really got the fact that nobody cared who you had been before you hit town." No wonder Dylan collapsed on the floor in amazed hilarity when he discovered that one of his folk heroes, the cowboy minstrel Ramblin' Jack Elliott, was actually a Jewish doctor's son from Brooklyn named Elliott Adnopoz.

Sam Shepard, chronicling Dylan's Rolling Thunder tour in 1975 (during which the singer appeared onstage with his face coated white—another "Bob Dylan mask"), picked up on his penchant for self-creation: "Dylan has . . . made himself up from scratch. That is, from the things he had around him and inside him. Dylan is an invention of his own mind." The construction of an American identity goes well beyond such theatrical strategies as adopting a less ethnic stage name or an alluring back-story for the tabloids. It's the great natural resource of a nation that has had to fashion itself from whole cloth, and it is plentiful enough to be used in myriad ways. As Shepard noted, Dylan was "not the first one to have invented himself, but he's the first one to have invented Dylan."

Among the Dylans Dylan has invented, his most famous incarnation, that of the mid-sixties poet-prophet, has become so indelible a part of his legacy that we tend to forget it was ultimately only one phase among many. The music critic Paul Nelson recalled that in that period, "the world used to follow [Dylan] around, just waiting for him to drop a cigarette butt. When he did they'd sift through the remains, looking for significance. The scary part is they'd find it—and it really would be significant." All well and good, but even the Delphic oracle is a role that must be learned, and can eventually be discarded just like those cigarette butts.

Certain critics, however, can't seem to relinquish the oracular fantasy. David Dalton is a prime example. Devoted to the "phantasmagoria of [Dylan's] great mid-'60s albums" and the "inner turmoil" they express, he has nothing but disdain for the down-home twang of *Nashville Skyline* and the contentment of *New Morning*. "It's as though we're seeing a form of what [Dylan] might have become had he stayed in Hibbing, taken over his dad's appliance store, married early girlfriend Bonnie Beecher or Echo Helstrom, and settled down with a bunch of kids," he shudders. The problem, for Dalton and his like-minded contemporaries, is that Dylan's inner turmoil (which reflected their own) was replaced by "turgid optimism," that the pop shaman now seemed to be peddling feel-good snake oil. It's true that the mid-sixties Dylan is a compelling character, and will likely remain our most enduring image of him. But the idea that he should have to play out in perpetuity the tired fantasies of aging hipsters is ludicrous.

Besides, who said a performer must inhabit every verse with absolute sincerity? What if Dylan were just trying out these stances, as artists do? What if he meant albums such as *Nashville Skyline* and *New Morning* as both optimistic *and* ironic, expressions of a point of view he'd like to believe in but isn't sure he can? And whoever said art has to be fashioned from lived experience in the first place? Hasn't the entire thrust of modernism and postmodernism been to challenge that notion? Does it make Dylan's voice any less "real" if he views songwriting, and the tradition behind it, through the lens of art, which is to say artifice?

If the role that artists and singers are asked to play is called Authenticity, then the ablest among them will deliver their lines right on cue. Art is one part inspiration, many parts imitation, and never a whole truth. This doesn't preclude genuine feeling—think of Dylan bemoaning Hattie Carroll's lonesome death or Sam Cooke foretelling "A Change Is Gonna Come." It simply means that in order to convey these feelings, the artist assumes different parts, taps into different selves. And Dylan has been spectacularly good at playing his many characters—whether the hardscrabble hobo, the righteous indicter of social injustices, the cooler-than-cool hipster with shimmering aureole and trademark Wayfarers, the contented country husband raising children and chickens, the womanizing rock star, the brimstone preacher, the encyclopedic radio DJ, or the itinerant blues statesman—perhaps because, to varying degrees, he has *been* every one of them.

It's not an either/or proposition. Some of Dylan's songs and performances no doubt did come from that "genuine Bob Dylan" we jealously preserve in our imaginations, while others lean heavily on pastiche. To a greater or lesser extent, Dylan's work has always combined authenticity and fakery, originality and appropriation and original appropriation. Does it matter to anyone but professors how his songs come into being, so long as they resonate? For my money, a good collage is more satisfying than a bad piece of original expression (if such a thing exists).

In *No Direction Home*, Joan Baez observed, "There are no veils, curtains, doors, walls, anything between what pours out of Bob's hand onto the page and what is somehow available to the people who are believers in him. Some people—*pfft*—not interested. But if you're interested, he goes way, way deep." Despite this direct connection, and the iconic status it has conferred on him, Dylan's music will never have the mainstream appeal of a Lady Gaga, Michael Jackson, or Taylor Swift. But for those who love the craggy edges in his singing, playing, and writing, no other singer-songwriter of his generation is as emotionally engaging. While acts from Peter, Paul and Mary to Adele have made hay with sweetened renditions of his music, Dylan himself delivers these songs in a voice that is flatly unsentimental—a mix of Delta bluesman, Will Rogers–style commentator, and mountain sage—and all the more authoritative for it. The paradox is that his mumbling, famously off-putting singing style lays bare the emotion behind the lyrics, in a way that the mellifluous and more overtly emotive approach adopted in many cover versions does not.

A related claim could be made for his performances in general, which range from the sublime to the frankly awful. As Clinton Heylin has written, "There is nobody I can think of in his league who has produced work as *bad* as Bob Dylan." In particular, Heylin has held up the so-called Never Ending Tour, the grueling round of concerts that Dylan has maintained since 1988, as "a perfect metaphor for Dylan's career: sprawling and messy, the highs jostling for attention with the many lows." But then, that's the point: unlike more polished musicians, who deliver reliable but predictable performances, Dylan has made a virtue of keeping his fans guessing. On any given night, he might be surly, or bored, or contrived, or simply indifferent. But he might also show up in a gold lamé suit and shake hands with the crowd, or treat it to some uncharacteristic banter, or sing a number he's never done before and isn't likely to repeat. He might also perform a song he's sung by rote thousands of times and somehow invest it with new life and energy, or else give the impression that he dimly heard the original ten years before and isn't quite sure how it goes. You just never know.

David Kinney, in *The Dylanologists*, notes that people have followed the Never Ending Tour "for years in the hopes of hearing something rare and wonderful, a moment when suddenly Dylan came alive and gave a song some new twist." As an artistic approach, it's exciting, and as a showbiz trick, it's brilliant. How better to maintain an active audience base over half a century? One can't help thinking of B. F. Skinner's operant conditioning experiments, in which a rat must press the bar an increasing number of times to be rewarded with a pellet.

Like Rimbaud or James Dean, Dylan has come to represent desires we often cannot name or define. Ever since "Blowin' in the Wind" went from being an off-the-cuff burst of bravado to the counter-culture's national anthem, he has consistently refused the role of spokesman for "his generation." Yet it was largely on the strength of his records and statements that his generation came to look upon both old conservatives and old liberals with a jaundiced eye, that it found miracle fabrics un-miraculous and split from split-level houses, that it took a particular dislike to authority ("For them that must obey authority / That they do not respect in any degree") and transitioned from the feel-good activism of the early sixties to the solipsistic hedonism of decade's end. The irony is that Dylan, simultaneously younger than that now and so much older, was already rejecting that generation by the time it came into full flower.

Even today, despite Dylan's boundless capacity to confound his audience, to elude their demands and anticipations, those demands keep coming. The more we try to make sense of the puzzle, the more he keeps moving the pieces around and bringing in new ones from out of nowhere. Just as we think we're in step with the New Dylan, he pulls the rug out. We call him poet and singer, prophet and phony, bard and sell-out, and he both embraces and shreds every one of those labels. We try to fit him into our own personal "Bob Dylan" mold, and he comes along to smash it. Over and over, he repeats what he said to Robert Shelton nearly sixty years ago: "When people believe that I am *this* or *that*, already there is a misunderstanding, a barrier between them and me," or what he scribbled in an early note to self: "whomever you think I am / I would suggest you reconsider." It ain't him, babe. And he ain't us.

THE COMPLICATED LITTLE GIRL

When André Breton proclaimed in 1922 that poetry "emanates more from the lives of human beings—whether or not they were writers—than from what they have written or from what we might imagine they could write," it is unlikely that the poet who later published under the name Laure, then nineteen and cloistered in the bourgeois family estate, would have got wind of it. Yet in many ways she was the embodiment of Breton's pronouncement. Indeed, most people, if they know of Laure at all, know her not so much for what she committed to paper as for her tortured, inspired relationships with several prominent French intellectuals, most notably the Surrealist-adjacent Georges Bataille. And though the publication of her *Collected Writings* clearly aims to correct that impression, its ultimate effect is only to reinforce it. By the time one emerges from this compilation of autobiographical and biographical sketches by and about her, of poems, scattered notes, and fevered letters, one can't help feeling that Laure's true masterwork was her ability to make others react to and remember her.

Which is not to say that Laure didn't take her writing seriously, or that we shouldn't either. On the contrary, poetry and autobiographical fragments were a way to exorcise otherwise inescapable demons, even though the very act of writing, said her nephew Jérôme Peignot, "contributed to giving her mental pain the intensity of a furnace." Rather than see literature as a path to glory or wealth, Laure produced much of her work in secret, apparently with little thought of publication (in this, she was no doubt truer to the Surrealist spirit than were most of her better-known fellows); even her lover Bataille saw almost none of her pages during their four years together. Only on her deathbed, at the age of thirty-five, did she reveal their existence, expressing the wish "that her testimony not remain uncommunicated . . . as only that which exists for others can have meaning." The task of bringing these texts to light fell to Bataille and Michel Leiris, another intimate of Laure's. That was in 1938, when family censorship kept most of them from being published. The first comprehensive volume of Laure's work in French finally appeared, thanks to Jérôme Peignot's efforts, in 1977, followed by a complete English translation, by Jeanine Herman, in 1995.

Born Colette Laure Lucienne Peignot in 1903, Laure spent most of her childhood and adolescence in her parents' estate in Dammarie, just outside Paris. Jérôme Peignot described Dammarie as "a pleasant place. In front of the house, a great lawn surrounded by stately chestnut trees slopes down to the Seine. One might think of Renoir or perhaps also Pissarro." But, he added, "rather than the extravagant luminosity of the Impressionists, it would be more accurate to evoke the false bourgeois tranquility painted by Vuillard."

Laure's childhood had in fact been anything but idyllic, and behind her own descriptions of it we can hear the restrictive admonishments and stony silences of the upper-middle class in post-World War I Europe. (One thinks of Laure's near-contemporary Leonora Carrington.) She wrote that her mother's situation "allowed her to close herself off in total distrust of anything that was not Family and in complete ignorance of anything that could be cheerful, active, engaging, lively, productive, or even simply human."

Laure's early years were further damaged by bouts of tuberculosis and, far more so, by the wartime deaths of her beloved father and three of her uncles—a calamity to which the not quite adolescent girl responded with a mixture of iciness and desperation:

> I forced myself to picture the faces of the cadavers but their names came to me in a song, a very cheerful tune that ended like this:
>
> They are dead, dead, dead
> André and Rémi . . .
> They are dead, dead, dead
> Papa, André, Lucien and Rémi . . .

After a long period of mourning, she

> thought it would be good to go to school. What had changed? Hadn't we been crying for months and months? Why not go out? But I was reprimanded, ashamed of my act, which was "heartless." So I stayed there with my mother whose sobs redoubled at each visit . . . There was something overwrought in all of this that did not suit me. I felt ashamed of my dry eyes and then atrocious remorse for not suffering enough.

This "Story of a Little Girl," as Laure called it, rehearses her main themes: revolt against weakness and dishonesty, rejection of the placid Catholicism of her milieu—a dismissal that itself takes on the tones of religious fervor—and disdain for socially conditioned attitudes. Most of all, it reveals an underlying belief in writing as the only means of personal salvation and worthwhile communication: "I felt horribly distant from all of them, capable of unravelling what each of them wanted, incapable of expressing my own reality to anyone in the world," she says of her neighbors in Dammarie.

As in her adult years, she did her writing in secrecy, like a private act of rebellion whose concealment made it all the sweeter. Secrecy—and its underlying feeling of mortification, of sin, of things that cannot be confessed—is essential to Laure's work. Describing her early puberty, she points to a duality that often results when a strong libido comes head-on against ramparts of shame and guilt: "Life soon managed to oscillate between these two poles: one sacred, venerated, which must be exhibited (my mother's contemplative demeanor after Communion); the other dirty, shameful, which must not be named." Laure was hardly the only woman of her time and background to internalize the schism between "archangel or whore," as she put it in one of her poems. Where she differed from many of the others was in her refusal to keep the two separate. Instead (and not unlike Bataille), she made of "sin" a religion unto itself, one to be practiced just as devoutly, fervently, and openly as her mother's more traditional obeisance to the Church.

Laure had direct experience of this duality in her adolescence, when she realized that the local priest, a "great friend of the family," was in the habit of sexually molesting her older sister. Her mother, whom she confronted with the facts, staunchly refused to believe them and instead accused her younger daughter of every perversion. She wasn't entirely wrong, for while the incident cemented Laure's hatred of organized religion and its manifold hypocrisies, it also stiffened her belief in an unbreakable link between the holy and the profane. One text in *The Sacred*, a collection of poems and fragments, borrows typically Bataillian accents to recount an orgiastic anti-Communion:

> The next day she climbed onto the altar and showed her ass to all the churchgoers and the priest, while raising the host, spread her thighs and inserted the host between them, then he licked this divine ass until the choirboy, kneeling in front of him, released his cock from between the lace and gilding, with blows of the censer and he swallowed the Holy Come that spurted

> into his face. Meanwhile, Laure, her ass provided with a sacred suppository, freed her belly and her life with wild cries and convulsions, shaking the grand altar to its foundations until it collapsed beneath her.

Seeking someone with whom she could communicate in the stifling atmosphere of her childhood home, Laure looked to those whose behavior and attitudes set them apart from the conventionality of her upbringing. As a young girl, she turned toward her brother, Charles, who enjoyed—and, for his sister, represented—a certain freedom from the strictures that their mother sought to impose; but Charles, "with his gluttonous and easy ways," was not someone Laure could truly "speak to." Later, it was Charles's wife, Suzanne, who attracted the eighteen-year-old's confidences, expressed in a series of passionate and sometimes rambling letters full of adolescent effusion and insecurity: "Don't pity me anymore, scold me—perhaps I've been too arrogant, but I cannot be content with mediocrity any longer," Laure wrote to Suzanne in 1922. "I love you with all my heart and I don't know how to tell you how touched I am by your patient tenderness for the complicated little girl I am."

But Laure's real break from her family, as well as her first relationship, did not come until she was twenty-two, when she fell in love with the novelist and Communist militant Jean Bernier. The relationship did not last long—Bernier was simultaneously involved with another woman—but for Laure it marked an affective and artistic breakthrough: "Do you understand," she wrote to her sister-in-law, "that this miracle [of feeling alive through writing] is embodied in him and also that he justifies the feeling that if everything that wanted to come to life in me, if all latent possibilities found their expression, it would be complete anguish, the height of anxiety—negation in exaltation."

The following year, partly in despair over Bernier, Laure attempted suicide, surviving only because the bullet ricocheted off a rib before it could reach her heart. The experience seems to have toughened her emotionally. In a farewell letter to Bernier written shortly afterward, she urged him to "refuse to accept *self-doubt* . . . A human being cannot doubt himself when he is following his own path. If he doubts, if he lowers his head, it's because an element foreign to strength, to his strength *to be spontaneously* is pulling him backward . . . Why do human beings refuse to be like plants—they want to be less, much less. They become rust."

Not long after this, Laure cut herself off from everyone, moved to Berlin, and began an abusive relationship with a wealthy, cultivated, and thoroughly depraved German doctor named Eduard Trautner, who kept her in grand style and regularly beat her, apparently with her consent. Recalling that period in *The Sacred*, she wrote: "I flung myself on a bed the way one flings oneself into the sea. Sexuality seemed separate from my real being. I had invented a hell, a climate in which everything was as far away as possible from what I had been able to foresee for myself. No one in the world could ever contact me, look for me, find me." Bataille, in his brief evocation of Laure's life, noted that during this period, Laure "dressed immaculately" in "black stockings, perfumes, and silk dresses by the great couturiers. She lived with Wartberg"—Trautner—"never went out, never saw anyone, stretched out on a divan. Wartberg brought her dog collars; he put her on a leash on all fours and lashed her with a whip like a dog. He had the face of a convict; he was a relatively older man, vigorous, refined. Once, he gave her a sandwich smeared with his shit."

From the sexual debasement of Berlin, Laure moved on to what her family saw as the political debasement of Communism. As a daughter of the upper bourgeoisie, she had been discouraged from associating with the domestics and laborers who daily serviced the household;

work, she was told, "made one ugly and dirty." Later, like many affluent rebels in the early thirties, she turned toward the Left, investing it with the same religious aura that had earlier marked her love for Bernier and her masochism with Trautner. She studied Russian at the prestigious Ecole des Langues Orientales in Paris, then moved to a garret in Moscow in an attempt to live like a proletarian. She even tried to spend the winter in an isolated peasant village. Yet, as Bataille recognized, her conviction was less political than psychological: "What dominated her was the need to give herself completely, and honestly. She wanted to become a militant revolutionary, yet her agitation was vain and feverish." She was, in any case, unprepared for the harshness of the Russian winter and its privations: soon after arriving among the muzhiks, she fell gravely ill and had to be brought home.

Laure's political activities did not end there, however. Back in Paris, she became the lover of Boris Souvarine, editor of the hardline Communist periodical *La Critique sociale,* which she helped finance. According to Bataille, it was also during this period that Laure would "seduce vulgar men and make love to them, even in the toilet of a train." Souvarine, with all the puritanism of a good Soviet, made it his mission to save her from this *nostalgie de la boue*, treating her "like an invalid, like a child," and being "more a father to her than a lover." When Bataille spent a weekend with the couple in 1934, he quickly realized that Laure's relationship with Souvarine was "poisoned."

It was not long after this that Bataille and Laure entered into a friendship that would soon develop into the most passionate affair of both their lives. Bataille was married at the time to the actress Sylvia Maclès (later the wife of the renegade psychoanalyst Jacques Lacan), but he was immediately seduced by Laure's implacable intensity. "From the first day, I felt a complete clarity between her and me. From the beginning she inspired unreserved trust," he later wrote. "No one has ever seemed to me as uncompromising and pure as she, or more decidedly 'sovereign,' and yet everything in her was devoted to darkness. Nothing came to light."

One can easily see what brought Laure and Bataille together: the theoretician of eroticism and sacrilege could not help responding to a woman of evident physical and intellectual appeal, who wallowed in the filth into which he occasionally dipped his big toe (all the while retaining about her an aura of moral purity), who absolutely refused to take anything lightly (Michel Leiris remarked that having a conversation with Laure was like "being on the edge of a blade"), and whose directness and intelligence were constant provocations. The character of their relationship can be glimpsed in Bataille's novel *Blue of Noon*, in which Laure is cast as "Dirty" to his "Troppmann" (the name taken from a celebrated spree murderer):

> In London, in a cellar, in a neighborhood dive—the most squalid of unlikely places—Dirty was drunk. Utterly so . . . As she stretched her long legs, she went into a violent convulsion. The place was crowded with men, and their eyes were getting ominous. Dirty clasped her naked thighs with both hands. She moaned as she bit into a grubby curtain.
>
> Her shoulders were bare to the point of indecency . . . She gave me a feeling of purity nonetheless. Even in her debauchery, there was such candor in her that I sometimes wanted to grovel at her feet. I was afraid of her . . . She was on the point of falling down. She began gasping for breath, panting like an animal; she was suffocating. Her mean, hunted look was driving me insane.

Over the next four years, until her early death from tuberculosis, Laure and Bataille pursued a liaison that was in many ways a communion of souls—one frequently undermined by her violence and jealousy and his "systematic, abundant" infidelities, but in which the exaltation of extremes so essential to both was given free rein. "What can be vaster than the gap through which two beings recognize each other, escaping the vulgarity and platitude of the infinite?" Bataille wrote shortly after her death. "Pain, terror, tears, delirium, orgy, fever, then death were the daily bread that Laure shared with me, and this bread leaves me the memory of a formidable but immense sweetness; it was a love eager to exceed the limits of things." As for Laure, while little in *The Collected Writings* suggests that she was ever truly content, she nevertheless seems to have found in Bataille a lover who could respond to her need for both communication and transcendence. One fragment puts it directly: "The God—Bataille / BATAILLE / To replace God."

I have said more about Laure's letters and autobiographical fragments than her poetry because, truth be told, I find her writings more compelling as the record of a life than as literature (compelling but somewhat disturbing: entering Laure's world is not a restful experience). The images in her poems of mutilation and decay, despair and putrefaction that no doubt fascinated Bataille today seem a bit shopworn. She is not above a few basic clichés—the "cynical prostitutes . . . with a great love in their hearts drowned in absinthe" who flit through the "Story of a Little Girl" are one example. Jeanine Herman's translation, while it credibly renders Laure's voice, occasionally stumbles. Her direct speech adheres so closely to the French that it's hard to imagine people actually talking that way, and she sometimes misses common idioms (for example, the expression *se regarder en chiens de faïence*—"to glare at one another"—is literally but incomprehensibly translated as "looking at each other like earthenware dogs"). As for Laure's political texts, the best one can say is that they show a sincere attempt at burning conviction, even if more often than not she seems to be examining her own state of mind rather than social inequities.

A few years before her death, Laure confessed to Bataille: "It is not happiness I seek, but a latent, effective, and positive strength—I know I fool people—some think I am already very strong, assured and confident . . . it is not what impresses others that will ever satisfy me . . . I know that I will never achieve any 'goal' because even if this were to happen, at that moment only one thing would matter to me—to go beyond what would already no longer be a goal but a stage." All these decades later, the endless refusal to be satisfied, to settle, to become rust, still shines through Laure's writings.

WHICH YEAR AT WHERE?

So much critical ink has been shed over *Last Year at Marienbad* (1961) that one might wonder whether the flood of commentary, once receded, would take the film along with it. Alain Resnais's second feature, based on Alain Robbe-Grillet's original screenplay, has been lavishly praised and royally slammed; awarded the Golden Lion at the Venice Film Festival and nominated for an Oscar, but also branded an "aimless disaster" by Pauline Kael; lauded by some as a great leap forward in the battle against linear storytelling and a worthy successor to Hoffmann, Proust, and Borges, dismissed by others as hopelessly old-fashioned.

The ambivalence is understandable. *Marienbad* blatantly toys with our expectations regarding plotline, character development, continuity, conflict, resolution—all those elements we've come to expect from a satisfying motion picture. Like its nameless hero, the film relentlessly pursues us with a barrage of assertions while giving us little to hold on to as convincingly true, until in the end, we, like Delphine Seyrig's equally nameless heroine, have only two choices: remain steadfast in our resistance to the seduction or just plain submit.

The plot is disarmingly simple. At a retreat for One Percenters located somewhere in Europe, a man (referred to in the screenplay as X, and played by Italian heartthrob Giorgio Albertazzi) tries to convince a woman (A, Seyrig's character) that they had fallen in love the previous summer, "in Karlstadt, Marienbad, or Baden-Salsa. Or even here in this salon." In his telling, the putative couple had planned to run away together, but she had asked him to wait one year. The woman at first refutes X's claim but is gradually swayed by his insistence. After several episodes of muted sparring between X and A's cooler-than-thou husband-guardian, M (Sacha Pitoëff), mainly over hands of the matchstick game Nim that M always wins, A finally agrees to leave with X.

So far, it's still the same old story, a fight for love and bragging rights. The devil, as always, lurks in the details. Indeed, the more evidence X provides as proof of veracity, the more discrepancies emerge, and the more the enigma thickens. As the film progresses, the image on-screen appears almost willfully to clash with X's voice-over description, sometimes prompting him to shout at it like an exasperated director with an unmanageable star. Incidents and settings frequently repeat, but their details change disconcertingly between one iteration and the next: A's remembered bedroom veers from bare to baroque; the hotel gardens sometimes boast a maze of shrubbery, sometimes grand alleys as stiff and straight as the gentlemen's tuxedos. (Resnais obtained this effect by shooting at three different palaces, none actually located in Marienbad.) Added to the narrator's stalkerlike pursuit of the reticent heroine, these inconsistencies imbue the film with an atmosphere of uncertainty, instability, and threat.

The ambivalence that greeted the film, and that so shapes its content, also extends to its two main creators, ideal interlocutors ultimately speaking at cross-purposes. At the time of their meeting in 1960, they would have appeared the perfect match: Alain Resnais had just shaken up the film world, and cinematic convention, with his feature debut, *Hiroshima mon amour* (1959), while Alain Robbe-Grillet's four novels to date (*The Erasers, The Voyeur, Jealousy, In the Labyrinth*) had outraged scores of critics and established him as spokesperson for the *nouveau roman*, a brand of fiction in which plot is implied through objective description rather than divulged through in-depth character analysis. Introduced by Resnais's producers, the director and the scenarist quickly found much common ground between them, including a shared fascination with form over story line. "The question of defining an anecdote was something for later: the important thing was in the telling," Robbe-Grillet commented in an interview about their collaboration. "As long as the kinds of form were agreed on, we'd be able to think up the subject." They also shared a taste for imbricating invention and reality: Robbe-Grillet had been trained as an engineer, and his novels often dwell on minute details of buildings and landscape; Resnais had spent the decade before *Hiroshima* making documentaries with the emotional range of fiction, including lyrical meditations on van Gogh and *Guernica*, and the much acclaimed *Night and Fog* (1955), a nightmare tour of Nazi concentration camps scripted by the novelist and Holocaust survivor Jean Cayrol. Mirroring Robbe-Grillet's passion for architecture, another of Resnais's documentaries, *Toute la mémoire du monde* (1956), snakes through the labyrinth of the Bibliothèque Nationale, both celebrating the library's recesses and providing a nonfiction pendant to *Marienbad*'s numerous tracking shots of the sumptuous hotel corridors. After an inspiring first conversation, Robbe-Grillet drafted four proposals for Resnais; the director selected the most "sentimental and austere" as the best vehicle for their formal concerns.

On the one hand, *Marienbad* draws quite naturally on its cocreators' prior accomplishments. Like *Hiroshima*, it weaves a hypnotic network of repeated phrases and recurrent visual, musical, and narrative motifs. And as in *Hiroshima*, it stages a prolonged tug-of-war between two unnamed protagonists, he wooing her from a rival love interest with a psychoanalyst's perseverance, she caught between resistance and surrender—both films culminating in a virtual "transfer of affect." Like Robbe-Grillet's novels, meanwhile, *Marienbad* furnishes only the constituent parts of a story, leaving the viewer responsible for piecing them together. And like the novels—*Jealousy* (1957) being a prime example—it introduces into the mix distinct undertows of murder and violence, as well as telling variants that constantly upend whatever certainties we think we've gained. *Jealousy*, moreover, rehearses the triangular dynamic of *Marienbad*, including the watchful husband and the use of the initial A to designate the heroine.

At the same time, the film betrays some significant divergences between the two men's visions, perhaps accounting in part for the ineffable tension between the protagonists on-screen, as well as between what we see and what we hear. Robbe-Grillet later stressed how the writing of *Marienbad* benefited from some stimulating disagreements; yet at first, it was mainly he who carried the day, while Resnais's suggestions—such as introducing the outside world via references to current events, or making Seyrig's character pregnant—were mostly discarded. Robbe-Grillet then delivered a screenplay so detailed, down to indications of soundtrack and camera movement, that the director confessed to feeling like a mere "robot" in the first weeks of shooting. In the end, however (as intimated in his introduction to the published screenplay, and more explicitly aired in later comments), Robbe-Grillet was taken aback by certain of Resnais's interpretations, as if once established on the set, the director regained control of the project despite the author's best efforts to constrain him.

Among the more notable changes is the score, which the scenarist prescribed as music "to set one's teeth on edge . . . with percussive elements [such as] footsteps, isolated notes, shouts," but which in the film is dominated by a gravid, liturgical pipe organ heavily indebted to Wagner and the symphonies of Louis Vierne. (The composer was Delphine Seyrig's brother Francis, Resnais's last-minute choice after Messiaen turned him down, and in the event a wise move.) Nor did Robbe-Grillet appreciate the cast, finding Seyrig in particular unsuited for the character he fantasized. Perhaps most drastically, Resnais complexifies the screenplay's clear indication that X is rescuing A from a comfortable but stifling existence. By numerous subtle and not-so-subtle details, the visuals seem to favor the heroine's point of view, almost defending her against Robbe-Grillet's identification with X, giving her an autonomy and independence of mind out of register with the author's objectifying gaze. Robbe-Grillet called *Marienbad* "the story of a persuasion," in which the hero offers the woman "a past, a future, and freedom." In Resnais's realization of it, things are not nearly so simple.

No doubt Robbe-Grillet also objected to the level of stylization. While both men had envisioned a film characterized by "ritual deliberation, a certain slowness, a sense of the theatrical," one senses that Resnais took this further than Robbe-Grillet had expected. Did the novelist share, for instance, the director's love of Louis Feuillade's serial melodramas, his desire to capture in *Marienbad* "a certain style of the silent cinema [and] re-create that atmosphere"? One thing that can't have pleased Robbe-Grillet much, given his avowed penchant for S&M, is Resnais's use of silent-film conventions to deflate what had been scripted as a brutal rape fantasy into something so mannered as to appear comic. Resnais had even tried to obtain old-fashioned film stock to get the "halo" effect typical of silents, and his use of overexposure and exaggerated gestures is no doubt a way of compensating for its unavailability. (For the sharp-eyed observer, Resnais throws in another bit of cinema tradition: a ghostly profile of Alfred Hitchcock, incongruously appearing at screen right at about eleven minutes and thirty seconds—a nod to the Master of Suspense and his famous cameos, as well as a hint that *Marienbad* is, at bottom, a mystery.) The protagonists, too, seem in higher relief on-screen than in the author's visualization. While Albertazzi is comparatively bland, handsome in a disposable sort of way, the viewer's memory is indelibly marked by Seyrig with her strict black bob, so distinct from the bleached perm she sports in most films, and by Pitoëff—described in the screenplay simply as "tall, gray-haired, very elegant"—with his Nosferatu stare and face so gaunt it might have been caught in a trouser press. Sacha Vierny's photography contributes equally to the sense of artificiality, glazing the visuals with a patina of hieratic stillness, much like the fashion photos of Helmut Newton or Philippe Halsman in vogue at the time—and perfectly in sync with A's over-the-top Chanel and Evein gowns.

Though *Marienbad* is generally considered a love story, it is perhaps the most rigidly codified seduction ever filmed, with nary a hair out of place. X pursues A with B-movie persistence, but his ardor seems more focused on winning her over than on satisfying his passion: one can barely imagine them kissing, let alone making love. For a seducer, at times he seems patently cruel, his face betraying a kind of predatory hardness. Seyrig, whether disputing X's account of their past rendezvous or acquiescing to it, rarely seems to lose her composure, hardly rippling the stuffy atmosphere even when crying out or dropping a glass. Oddly, it is the preternaturally self-possessed Pitoëff who provides the film's one moment of actual tenderness, when he recognizes—perhaps even before she does—that A is about to leave him, bearing out the adage about those who are lucky at cards.

Like most art, *Marienbad* is ultimately about its own experience, the true dialogue occurring not between characters but between maker and audience. Robbe-Grillet's well-known comment that the "entire story of *Marienbad* happens neither in two years nor in three days, but exactly in one hour and a half"—the duration of the film—could in this regard be said of any cinematic work. But whereas most movies give at least the illusion of progress and resolution, here the story line is unapologetically elliptical, the spa and its guests hermetically sealed in "a perpetual present." The midnight chime we hear at the beginning of the film is quite literally the same as the one that ends the stage- and screenplay, in an eternal loop that brings the story back to its starting point and leaves us, like the seduced (and abandoned?) A, "losing our way forever in the stillness of night."

It is this constant dance of seduction and evasion that makes *Last Year at Marienbad* so challenging, engaging, and contemporary more than half a century after its premiere. On the one hand, the film constantly thwarts our efforts at rational interpretation, even as it dares us to keep trying. But at the same time, both Resnais and Robbe-Grillet have repeatedly stressed the very simple key to understanding and enjoying the work: just watch it. Let yourself be carried along by the music, the rhythms of Albertazzi's slightly stagey voice-over, the sinuosity of the tracking shots down the grand hotel corridors. *Marienbad* appears "difficult" if we try to impose a traditionally logical and chrono-logical structure on the flow of sounds and images—though perhaps less difficult now that so many films have taken their cue from it: Chris Marker's *La Jetée* (1962), Stanley Kubrick's *The Shining* (1980), Christopher Nolan's *Memento* (2000), and Cameron Crowe's *Vanilla Sky* (2001) immediately come to mind. But boiled down to its essence, nothing could be more self-evident, or more personal. "I don't think of [*Marienbad*] as an enigma," the director once told an interviewer. "Each spectator can find his own solution. But it won't be the same solution for everyone." Against a stiffly regulated backdrop located in a purely fabricated space, Resnais ushers us through the unpredictable and manifold corridors of human memory and desire.

WHOEVER IS WITH ME IS AGAINST ME

"He had 7 yachts, 127 automobiles, and that is little compared to his women," Francis Picabia's last wife wrote of him in 1949, with the painter's grinning complicity. Spanish and Cuban on his diplomat father's side, related through his mother to the conservative Parisian haute bourgeoisie, Picabia was born into a life of privilege in 1879 and, by virtually all accounts, he never grew up. The boy's mother died when he was seven, leaving him wanting for nothing except a stable emotional environment; the "womanless" home in which he was raised by his father, grandfather, and uncle offered comfort and culture but little warmth. In adulthood, with the carelessness of abundance taken for granted, Picabia passed through countries, acquisitions, friends, wives, lovers, artistic styles, and ideas as if they were all his private playground, quickly tiring of the previous flash enthusiasm and always eager for more, more, more.

Like Marcel Duchamp, his lifelong accomplice, rival, and fellow jester at the court of High Modernism, Picabia stands as both an indispensable entry in the avant-garde index and one of those Teflon eccentrics to whom the available categories never quite stick. But where Duchamp's life traces a *reductio ad absurdum* of personal wants, at least on the surface, Picabia's often seems an endless quest for newer and bigger pleasures. Germaine Everling, the painter's companion of sixteen years—the most acute commentaries come, fittingly, from his wives and mistresses, who saw right through him even as they succumbed to his charms—remarked that he had "a great thirst for events . . . little matter to him under what form they presented themselves: women, houses, automobiles, pets." And she relates how one day Picabia bought a country mechanic's garage on a whim, moved lock, stock, and barrel into the upper floor, and made a go of managing the repair shop—until the novelty wore off and he moved back to the capital.

Episodes such as these (and they are legion) have long fueled the common perception of Picabia as the dilettante's dilettante. But there is also a darker, more measured, more anxious side to his restless personality, and it is in his poems and aphorisms, rather than his copious plastic output, that this anxiety allowed itself freest expression. Marc Lowenthal, the editor and translator of *I Am a Beautiful Monster: Poetry, Prose, and Provocation**—the first comprehensive volume in English of Picabia's writings—suggests an explanation: writing was what Picabia did when he was unable to paint, either through circumstance or, more often, psychological impediment. In other words, and somewhat tautologically, the writings reflect the malaise that spawned them. This thesis has been floated by some of Picabia's biographers, who have described how the painter latched onto the pen when he couldn't wield the brush. But here the combination of Lowenthal's pertinent glosses and a generous helping of illustrative texts makes for one of the most persuasive arguments yet advanced that there was more behind the clown mask than just a clown.

It is, admittedly, a hard mask to penetrate. Picabia's best-known work, visual as well as verbal, is characterized by a fierce devil-may-care smirk that dares the viewer to take it, or anything else, seriously. A large part of its effect, which charmed the rebellious younger generation even as it infuriated most of the painter's contemporaries, comes from its refusal to be pinned down, its spirit of disregard that snubbed both labels and rules. This disregard applied not solely to his

---

* MIT Press, 2007.

art: called up for service during World War I, Picabia used his family connections to get sent on a vague mission to Cuba, which he then abandoned once his ship docked in Manhattan (an act of desertion that made him avoid France for the next two years). There he joined his old friend Duchamp, along with Man Ray, Alfred Stieglitz, and the unclassifiable Baroness Elsa von Freytag-Loringhoven, to develop the cluster of ideas and works retroactively dubbed New York Dada.

Until this point, the former child prodigy and Arts Décoratifs student had produced derivative canvases that by turns aped Impressionism, Fauvism, Futurism, and Cubism. He now began exploring, partly under Duchamp's influence, the visual motifs for which he is best known: precisely rendered engine parts and hardware items sporting titles such as *Amorous Parade* and *Shining Vagina*, which both translated the painter's lifelong ambivalence toward women and provoked a gratifying scandal among the public. Still, when later asked the inevitable question of what he had done during the war, his only answer was, "I was bored to hell."

After a year of New York high life, even Picabia the consummate hedonist had had enough, and he and his first wife, the writer Gabrielle Buffet, moved to Barcelona in the summer of 1916. It was during this period that the painter first turned to writing poems, one of which contains what might be a backward glance at his recent American experience:

> Everywhere men and women with music I enjoy
> publicly or in secret
> unleash their sterile passions.
> Opium.
> Whisky.
> Tango.

This poem is from *Fifty-Two Mirrors* (1917), Picabia's first collection of verse, which in the words of his biographer William Camfield "mirror[s] Picabia's response to the conditions of his life—sometimes clearly but in other instances so darkly that even the most sympathetic reader cannot penetrate their veiled, perverse reflections." This sense of fragmented depiction, mixing clarity with opacity, is a staple of the modernist aesthetic, but in Picabia's case the contrasts have less to do with literary technique than with his own conflicting impulses. The mirrors are trained almost exclusively on the author, and the glints they give off are not just for effect: in the present case, Picabia was clearly no stranger to sterile passions and "tangos," and behind the shorthand "Opium" lies a drug habit that would dog the painter for the next decade and more.

It was also in Barcelona that Picabia founded the journal *391,* which would prove one of the most influential of the avant-garde periodicals. Between 1917 and 1924, it was a testing ground for various experimental currents and—after Picabia's fabled meeting with Tristan Tzara—a primary mouthpiece for Dada. More than anything, *391* showcased its editor's own jottings, providing an arena for his bolder literary experiments, including samples of automatic writing that predate by several months André Breton and Philippe Soupault's seminal *The Magnetic Fields* of 1919. It also served as a kind of blog *avant la lettre*, whimsically reporting on the doings of Picabia and his friends ("Max JACOB declares that his ass is hysterical") and on whatever else came into his head ("Cubism is a cathedral of shit"). *391* has been called a "magazine in transit," and understandably so: less than a year after moving to Spain, Picabia was back in New York, the first four issues under his arm. Later that year he returned to Barcelona and Paris, then in February 1918 joined Gabrielle and their children in Switzerland. The magazine's successive mastheads, with their fluctuating editorial addresses, track his rambling itinerary.

Picabia's main reason for heading to Switzerland was to undergo treatment for a nervous breakdown: not only had he gone back to living in the fast lane, but his marriage was faltering because of his addiction and his new involvement with Germaine Everling, whom he had met during a separation from Gabrielle. By the end of 1917, the painter was shuttling between his family and his lover, and when the Picabias settled in Gstaad, Everling, by pre-arrangement, took a hotel room in nearby Lausanne, making Picabia's attempts at a rest cure fairly pointless. On doctor's orders, Picabia severely curtailed his painting—and in a typical bit of perverseness dedicated one of his few watercolors of the time to that same physician—but he made up for it with a vastly increased outpouring of poems, many of which offer the same brooding self-reflection as the pieces in *Fifty-Two Mirrors*.

Nor was he content with the complications of merely two women in his life. Before leaving New York, he had indulged in a tryst with Isadora Duncan; and in Lausanne, all the while flitting between Buffet and Everling, he took up with a young artist—the affair ending when the woman's husband came after the feckless Casanova with a pistol. In the fall of 1918, when Picabia's doctor sent him to the spa town of Bex-les-Bains to avoid the Spanish flu pandemic, the painter took both his family and Everling with him and installed everyone in a suite of adjoining rooms.

Still, even Picabia's amorous parade fizzles next to the embroiled complexities and quicksand alliances of his involvement with Paris Dada. The catalyst was the painter's correspondence with Tristan Tzara, Dada's head theorist and publicist, in the summer of 1918. Shortly before this, Tzara had unveiled his "Dada Manifesto 1918" ("Every man must shout: there is great destructive, negative work to be done. Sweep, clean"), winning international renown among the disillusioned young artists and writers just emerging from the war. By early

1919, Picabia and Tzara had met in Zurich and collaborated on a new issue of *391*, and when Picabia settled back in Paris soon afterward, he began spreading the Dada gospel. Among those most eager to hear it were the young poets André Breton, Louis Aragon, and Paul Eluard, the kernel of the future Surrealist group, who had been experimenting with forms of poetry that mirrored what Tzara and Picabia were producing, and who were ripe for the scorched-earth assault the movement promised. Breton got to know Picabia at the end of 1919. When Tzara made his own migration to Paris the following month, taking over Everling's apartment (where Picabia was now living) and Breton's magazine *Littérature* in the process, the resulting concentration of energies unleashed one of the most rambunctious periods in the history of the avant-garde.

Dada got off to a rousing start in Paris with a series of provocative statements and performances, and at first Picabia was an eager participant—to a degree that even his avid young acolytes found taxing. "Each time a Dada demonstration was planned," Breton later recalled, "Picabia gathered us in his salon and *demanded* that each of us in turn come up with *ideas* for it." But true to form, Picabia also kept his distance from the collective shenanigans. Though he contributed a number of skits and manifestoes, he declined to perform them himself, leaving his junior colleagues to face the hecklers and rotten tomatoes as he watched from an upper box of the theater—"something to keep in mind," as Lowenthal dryly notes, "when reading a line such as 'Hiss, yell, smash my face in . . .'"

Despite these buffers, Dada is the context in which Picabia truly flourished, the one label that, notwithstanding, manages to keep at least a corner of itself attached to his oeuvre. Not only did it spur on the aggressive "anti-art" he was now producing (such as the painting *The Cacodylic Eye* in 1921, covered in his friends' graffiti and looking, as one critic put it, like "the interior of a pissoir"), but with its belligerent laughter and combative refusal of all standing values, Dada was the ideal petri dish for Picabia's virulent humor. Perhaps nowhere was this better exercised than in the painter's defenses of the much-stigmatized movement. When André Gide issued a condescending review of a Dada show, Picabia retorted, "Reading Gide aloud for ten minutes will give you bad breath." And when the poet Pierre Reverdy allegedly sent the Dadaists a violently insulting letter, he lost no time in publishing a rebuttal: "Monsieur Reverdy has just sent me an urgent letter . . . to tell me that he'd like to make me eat a bit of his shit. Dear Monsieur Reverdy, whom I do not have the honor of knowing, it seems to me that ever since you devoted your life to poetry you have been trying to make everyone eat a bit of your shit." Not too surprisingly, Picabia's subsequent "anti-Dada" writings are nearly indistinguishable from the ones written in support of Dada.

Nor was Picabia granted immunity from his own barbs. Many of the articles and aphorisms that he stuffed into *391* and other Dada periodicals targeted himself just as easily as they skewered his antagonists. When the Cubist painter Albert Gleizes sarcastically tarred Picabia as a "funny guy," Picabia appropriated the nickname as a byline. He also signed himself the "Cannibal," the "Alcoholic," the "Pickpocket," the "Idiot," and "Picabia who knows nothing, nothing, nothing"—all manifestations of what William Camfield calls his "'I screw myself' technique." As the painter wrote in 1920, "Whoever is with me is against me."

Given the personalities involved, it is no surprise that Dada soon began to sour, as the protagonists' conflicting agendas jostled to the fore. Angry with Tzara for trying to appropriate the Dada "brand" and with Breton for the moral gravitas he was seeking to impose on the movement, Picabia broke from his friends in May 1921, in a widely circulated newspaper interview: "The Dada spirit only really existed from 1913 to 1918 . . . after that, it became as uninteresting as the output of the Ecole des Beaux-Arts," he declared. "Dada, you see, was not serious, and . . . if some people now do take it seriously, it is because it is dead!"

Still, Picabia, who shifted allegiances as easily as he changed his socks, was not entirely through with his Paris comrades-in-arms. Having earlier sided with Tzara against Breton, he now sided with Breton against Tzara, once Breton himself had become disillusioned with Dada. The two men maintained cordial relations until 1924, when Breton launched the Surrealist movement as such, a movement that Picabia, as avant-godfather, felt should be under his leadership. A final showdown found the self-styled chiefs in Breton's studio—the rest of the group in attendance like spoils waiting to be claimed—trading insults until the painter, bested at his own game, finally stormed out. Soon afterward, he cranked up *391* one last time to lampoon the new Surrealist enterprise. Nevertheless, Breton retained enough admiration for Picabia to include some brief texts in his *Anthology of Black Humor* some two decades later, though he prefaced them by remarking that the "painter and poet" in Picabia was often eclipsed by the "much-less-inspired polemicist."

⋆

With equal parts acumen and shortsightedness, Breton's remark touches on two of the main elements to greet the reader of *I Am a Beautiful Monster*: the sporadic quality of Picabia's inspirations and (despite Breton's judgment) his consummate but uneven talent for invective and insult. While some of these texts display all the manic novelty of the avant-garde heyday, a number of others sound merely like random musings or unsupported bravado: the "provocations" touted in the subtitle might just as often be termed "prevarications." And behind many of them one can hear the self-congratulatory laughter of someone who knows he is being awfully clever, when it isn't the resentful snicker of a man who feels his genius is undervalued.

The anthology's chronological arrangement allows for a bird's-eye view of Picabia's literary development, further encouraged by Lowenthal's division of the texts into discrete periods. The first section, "Pre-Dada" (1917–1919), mainly includes darkly self-reflexive poetry with titles such as "Void," "Failed," and *The Mortician's Athlete*, and with allusions to the author's illnesses, chemical and sexual addictions, peripatetic existence, and overall dissatisfaction with life and lot. At times these writings amount to no more than juvenile pouting: "A modern society woman is an almost masculine stupidity" or "I loathe Cézanne's painting it bores me." But elsewhere a surprising self-knowledge peeps through the bluster. One poem from 1917, written during a separation from Gabrielle Buffet, confesses: "I have excuses / And lack strength and courage," while a short prose text from a few years later allows that "My only goal is a silkier life and an end to my lying."

In the texts from the Dada period proper (1919–1921), Breton's "much-less-inspired polemicist" takes center stage. This section contains some of Picabia's most quoted utterances and suggests a man fully at home in the chaos that he helped to foment. The manifestoes pound home the movement's nihilistic message, in an odd (and similarly repetitive) anticipation of 1970s punk. "Dada . . . is like your idols: nothing / like your politicians: nothing / like your heroes: nothing," rants Picabia's most famous contribution to the genre. Similarly, the poems he wrote during this period, collected in books such as *Thoughts Without Language*, *Unique Eunuch*, and the celebrated *Jesus Christ Rastaquouère* (which garnered praise even from the curmudgeonly Ezra Pound), ratchet up the tone, introducing a sharper sense of cruelty and crudity:

I'm going to whip your senses . . .
I smother the pussy enveloping my hand
I don't really know why these scenes resemble rags.
I kiss your mouth while vomiting . . .

Still, after a while what one mainly hears is the difficulty of sustaining an effective attack. How many times can one hector an audience and still keep its ear? This was the problem that tormented Breton and his friends, who retreated from the sterility of Dada's wasteland and began exploring the more verdant byways that ultimately led to Surrealism.

Picabia, meanwhile, chose simply to leave the building. After his break with Dada, he spent the late 1920s and 1930s living it up on the Côte d'Azur, either in a castle he built for Everling and their son near Cannes or on one of his several houseboats. He consorted with the rich and indolent, hosting fabulous galas at the casino in the evenings and motoring around by day in one of his 127 deluxe autos. His artwork, once joyously scandalous, now became (in Lowenthal's words) an "outpouring of figurative and abstract kitsch." Practically his only writings from this period are sour-grapes retorts to art critics, who had gotten used to the Dada provocateur and now damned him for his conservative twist: "If there is an artist too different from the others, a poor wretch who shows off, there is nothing to do but bully him, cut him down . . . [or else] they'll punish him even better: they'll stop talking about him!"

The final sections of the book, covering the period before World War II through the painter's death in 1953, evince a bitter retrenchment—manifest in Picabia's socially regressive politics, in his art, and in his poetry, which abandons bravado for previously unsounded notes of reticence and fear. The breathtaking egotism of the earlier volumes gives way to an apprehensive topicality about the impending war, even to a pathos of transparent emotional neediness:

If you wanted, completely naked, I would grow old
with your smile, hands on your breasts.

Whatever you do, don't throw me into the void!

These lines, from the aptly titled "Sentimental Poem," were most likely written for Olga Mohler, the Picabias' young nanny who became the painter's third wife in 1940—while Everling, who had weathered one too many of these dalliances, quit the household for good. The marriage to Olga, like its predecessors, seems to have run over its own share of potholes and inspired many of Picabia's late writings, some of them among the most rudely acerbic of his entire oeuvre.

By the time World War II broke out, the effusiveness that had characterized so much of Picabia's life shrank to almost nothing. The fabulous fortune dwindled, the yachts and fancy cars were sold off. In place of houseboats and casinos, the Picabias spent the war in a cramped apartment and got around by bicycle. In 1945, the perpetual nomad and world traveler came full circle and returned to live in the once-opulent apartment of his childhood, which bad real estate transactions had by now reduced to a single studio. Even his writings reflect this diminishment: Picabia's final collections, sometimes composed of no more than a few sentences (and not necessarily by him), were issued by a fledgling publisher in editions of fewer than fifty copies. As the Dada joker confessed in one of his last poems, "life has worn out / my hope / and no longer amuses me."

But fortunes change, and at this point Picabia's place in the history of modernism is assured. His influence on later currents such as Pop and Conceptual Art is palpable; and when we review the cultural history of his time, it is often Picabia's quick-witted tartness that exposes just how bland most of his contemporaries could be. Marc Lowenthal has done a superb job of organizing the painter's writings into a fairly coherent whole, and his introductions to the various groupings set the context as well as can be expected (though a little more biographical background would have been welcome). MIT Press has also designed the book so as to suggest at least some of the originals' typographic cacophony. As to the translations, while one could quibble with a few of the choices—stage hands use spotlights, not "projectors"; one plays solitaire, not "patience"; "let's always try" (*essayons toujours*) could more idiomatically be rendered "let's give it a shot"; and so on—in the main Lowenthal matches Picabia gripe for snipe.

There are also some interesting revelations to be noted between the lines of verse and commentary, such as the distinct accents of homosexuality that surface in a number of these writings—could the legendary womanizer have been overcompensating?—and the hitherto unreported extent to which Picabia borrowed, not to say plagiarized, from prior sources. Lowenthal highlights two main "inspirations" for Picabia's aphorisms, Nietzsche's *The Gay Science* (one of the few books the painter read with any attention) and the quotations pages of the Larousse dictionary, and he demonstrates how this form of appropriation fit into Picabia's aesthetic. Lowenthal could have taken the discussion further—he neglects the important precursor of Lautréamont's *Poésies*, which made similar use of maxims by Pascal and La Rochefoucauld, and which Picabia (who surely knew the book) might have seen as a go-ahead for his own pilferage—but the parallels that he does draw with Nietzsche and others engage the reader in a more fruitful dialogue with Picabia's texts than would otherwise be possible.

So why can't I finally muster more enthusiasm for this book? Because for all of their sharpness and invention, these writings too seldom reach past mere cleverness or navel-gazing: true self-revelation, if it is to avoid being embarrassing or just plain tedious, demands empathy, depth, and restraint—qualities not normally associated with Picabia's work. Instead, there is a tossed-off, scattershot quality to his darts, which miss as often as they hit, or strive way too hard for effect. And perhaps more than anything, one feels from start to finish a kind of desperation in these texts, an undercurrent of uselessness that is far more dispiriting than the painter's defiant reiterations of "nothing, nothing, nothing." As he once put it, and much more tellingly, "Between my head and my hand, there is always the face of death."

One might rightly object that desperation was part and parcel of Dada's mission. One might also point to similar notes of demoralization in the writings of Tzara, Breton, Arp, and their fellows. But Breton, for one, never lost faith in that "certain point of the mind" at which the debilitating contradictions of the human condition might be resolved. As for Tzara, even his "great destructive" prescription for a clean sweep allowed one to imagine something better once the garbage of the centuries had been cleared away. The proof is that he eventually joined up with the Surrealist project in the 1930s, and later militated with the Communist Party—at a time when Picabia was busily damning the leftists as "poor revolutionaries, made in series," and sneering at the very notion of social reform.

I imagine that reading this anthology is not unlike the experience of knowing Picabia himself: alternately exhilarating and exasperating, the truly inspired pronouncements counterbalanced by the merely obnoxious ones. Ultimately, this collection might reveal more about the beautiful monster than it intended, for by an odd but appropriate paradox, it bespeaks a more complex figure than posterity has retained even as it undercuts the legends that earned Picabia that posterity. As the outsized ejaculations of the Dada period slip into the relative quietude of the painter's final decades, the book becomes an exercise in declining vigor and diminishing returns. The recurrences and borrowings in the first sections at least participate in a rabid promiscuity of ideas, as if the sheer velocity of expression and event didn't leave time to check whether something had been said before, or by whom; but the last hundred or so pages make you feel like you've been cornered at a party by a bitter also-ran who endlessly reprises his best lines of yore to hide the sad truth that he has nothing new to say. By the end of this voluminous tome—with its obsessive repetitions and phenomenal self-absorption, its private jokes and petty bickering, its vindictiveness and magnificence—one cannot help recalling another of Picabia's self-mocking nicknames, trotted out, like virtually all his *bons mots*, time and time and time again: Francis the failure.

LIVES BEHIND LIVES: BIOGRAPHY AS AUTOBIOGRAPHY

The hullabaloo that some years ago greeted Edmund Morris's *Dutch,* a biography of Ronald Reagan that employs (among other controversial devices) an invented autobiographical narrator, highlighted both the writer's and the reader's ambivalent attitudes toward biographers stepping into the frame of their subject's life. Like Hollywood's fabled fourth wall, a first-person intrusion in the fantasy of omniscient history remains a source of discomfort, a reminder that we are being led not by the absolute, reconstructed truth, but by someone's very particular viewpoint. At the same time, there is a fascination with the process of biography, a sense that if we are allowed in to the writer's journey of discovery (mostly a rather plodding journey, as any biographer can attest), we will somehow get closer to the life, even share in its recreation.

It's easy to understand the biographer's desire to recount their odyssey. Who wouldn't, after three, five, ten, twenty years spent laboring over a single project, want to complain about the thankless research, the impasses and self-doubts, the intractable widows and executors, or to crow about the moments of affirming insight and sheer brilliant luck? And of course, many do: often in the wake of a new biography, articles and interviews are given to any medium that will listen, detailing, sometimes excruciatingly, the triumphs and travails that occurred between concept and publication. But in a few cases, those occurrences are made part and parcel of the finished work itself, a parallel narrative dogging the ostensible life story like a wily predator, sometimes even yanking the biographical subject offstage to remind us that, hey, someone's working hard here to get you all this information, and believe me, friend, it's no cakewalk. The result is a kind of meta-biography, a tale-within-a-tale that sometimes becomes more compelling, more central than the tale itself.

There are precedents to Morris's approach, of course, even among the earliest examples of the genre. James Boswell, in his celebrated, and still exemplary, portrait of Samuel Johnson, loses few opportunities to remind us that he is Johnson's—well, his Boswell. A century and a half later, Gertrude Stein reinvented her companion Alice B. Toklas, so that the latter's supposed *Autobiography* might read to all the world as an objective, if wholly flattering, third-person portrait of Gertrude Stein. And in 1934, A. J. A. Symons set the tone for this sort of forensic meta-research in *The Quest for Corvo: An Experiment in Biography*, which says less about the elusive Frederick Rolfe than about Symons's tenacious pursuit of him.

In modern times, an exemplar of this kind of biography is no doubt Ian Hamilton's ultimately frustrating quest *In Search of J. D. Salinger.** Hamilton, fresh from his success as Robert Lowell's intrepid chronicler, decided to accord the same treatment to America's most recalcitrant novelist, only to find that neither his sleuthing skills nor his appeals to the writer's presumed vainglory were able to penetrate the cloak of silence that Salinger had been weaving around himself for the previous two decades.

It was not for lack of trying: Hamilton contacted Salinger and his extended family; weathered several stingingly dismissive replies, most notably from Salinger himself; interviewed numerous former acquaintances; visited the schools and major sites (including an attempted visit to Salinger's walled-in home in Cornish, New Hampshire); read

* Random House, 1988.

everything, published and unpublished, that he could get his hands on. His aim was to focus on Salinger's life and career before the author's self-imposed seclusion in 1965, and despite the many obstacles put in his path, he eventually sent his publisher, Random House, a manuscript that he intended to call *J. D. Salinger: A Writing Life*—as complete a traditional biography as could be written under the circumstances. "It was not," he admits, "really the book I wanted it to be. It was too nervous and respectful, and in many ways disabled by my anxiety to assure Salinger that I was not a rogue. But it was workmanlike, it had far more facts about the man than you could find anywhere else, it had . . . something of his tone of voice, his presence. And in its literary-critical aspects, it did, I thought, have some useful things to say about the relationship between the author's life and work. It was *all right*." The book's one saving grace, in its author's eyes, the thing that kept it to this side of "all right" and that preserved the protagonist's tone of voice, was its copious use of Salinger's unpublished letters, obtained by dint of extensive digging and a few lucky breaks. While not making up for the many unavoidable gaps, these quotations provided the necessary heft, authority, and above all timbre that would ensure the volume (in Hamilton's own assessment) "a quiet, if not thoroughly reclusive, life in campus bookstores."

But even this was not to be, for a threatened lawsuit by Salinger prompted, in Hamilton's case, the enforced removal of virtually all his unpublished quotations, and in the larger arena, a drastic reevaluation of the fair use laws. Anyone who has been in a similar position can sympathize with Hamilton's lament, when then forced to paraphrase Salinger's quotations, that "in almost every instance, I was deadening his language; I was making him seem duller than he was. Whose interests did this serve?"

Logical assumption would dictate that Hamilton then fell back on his only remaining option: an improvised Plan B that had him madly retrieving his research notes, plugging them in to the manuscript, and turning his intended biography into the version we now know as *In Search of J. D. Salinger.* The reality, however, is that Hamilton had envisioned such a book from the start, and the real Plan B was in fact the more traditional biography he initially sent in to Random House, and that the publisher eventually rejected. "I had it in mind to attempt not a conventional biography—that would have been impossible—but a kind of *Quest for Corvo*, with Salinger as quarry," he tells us at the outset:

> According to my outline, the rebuffs I experienced would be as much part of the action as the triumphs—indeed, it would not matter much if there were no triumphs. The idea—or one of the ideas—was to see what would happen if orthodox biographical procedures were to be applied to a subject who actively set himself to resist, and even to forestall, them . . . It would be a biography, yes, but it would also be a semispoof in which the biographer would play a leading, sometimes comic, role.

His design, in other words, was to set himself against Salinger—as hunter and prey, intrepid adventurer and guarded treasure—in a game of cat-and-mouse played out before our avid eyes.

Eschewing the biographer's traditional goals ("it would not matter much if there were no triumphs"), Hamilton went right to the heart of what, in reality, lies beneath the skin of virtually all biographies, though generally it remains at a deeper layer: a desire to enter into a privileged, not to say exclusive, relation with the subject; to insert oneself, retrospectively if need be but lastingly, into the subject's works and days. For Hamilton, this desire vis-à-vis Salinger quite naturally began with a reading of *The Catcher in the Rye*: "*The Catcher* was the book that taught me what I ought already to have known: that literature can speak *for* you, not just to you. It seemed to me 'my book.' It was something of a setback when I eventually found out that I was perhaps the millionth adolescent to have felt this way."

Throughout the book, Hamilton maintains a running dialogue, even a rivalry, with his "biographizing alter ego," his "constant companion," the driven pro who dismisses our hero's scruples about Salinger's right to privacy and who remains "merely eager to get on with the job." To the Hamilton who places certain portions of Salinger's life off-limits and who stops to wonder, "At what point does decent curiosity become indecent?," the biographer responds with an impatient wave of the hand, along with a reminder that Salinger is a public figure, therefore fair game, and that their only task is to collect the facts, any facts, from any source. Even when our ambivalent narrator finds the tables turned on him, during a visit to the Harry Ransom research center in Austin, Texas, his alter ego remains intractable:

> While I was waiting for the Salinger file to be hauled up from the vaults, I thumbed through the library's card index. Needless to say, the first name I looked up was HAMILTON, IAN (1938–). Even Texas couldn't be *that* comprehensive. But it was; to my horror, more than a dozen letters were listed under my defenseless name. Why, anyone could just walk in and . . . My companion indicated that the Salinger dossier was now sitting on desk three.

It is this ongoing dialogue with his other half that supplies Hamilton with a forum for some crucial debates about the underlying nature of the biographer's task, as well as the realization of some unpleasant home truths faced (or studiously ignored) by any serious biographer: that the biographer is in a predatory relationship with the subject, regardless of whether that subject is living or dead; that catching the protagonist "in the act"—any act—can make one feel "rather as policemen do, or torturers, when the confession finally gets signed." And more than this, that behind most serious biographical research—not strictly-for-the-cash commission work, but thorough, dedicated labor that sometimes takes decades—is a need that ultimately says more about the author's biography than the subject's.

Coming to the end of his disheartening battle against both Salinger and the copyright laws, and of his progressive disenchantment with Salinger himself, Hamilton ruefully admits:

> When I really ask myself how this whole thing began, I have to confess that there was more to it than mere literary whimsy. There was more to it than mere scholarship. Although it will seem ludicrous, perhaps, to hear me say so now, I think the sharpest spur was an infatuation, an infatuation that bowled me over at the age of seventeen and which it seems I never properly outgrew. Well, I've outgrown it now.

I wonder how many practicing biographers can read such a statement without tasting an acrid tang of recognition.

★

A similar sense of wistfulness pervades Charles Nicholl's *Somebody Else: Arthur Rimbaud in Africa 1880–91,* a recreation of Rimbaud's legendary decade in Africa as a gun runner and entrepreneur.* While all biography

* Jonathan Cape, 1997.

on some level involves following in the subject's footsteps, Nicholl takes the process literally, living in and traveling through the places that Rimbaud haunted during his final trek toward "luminous ordinariness" (in the author's nicely turned phrase). What he finds, not surprisingly, is that the road is somewhat rockier than he had anticipated.

Like Hamilton, Nicholl sets out to recount his own journey in the wake of his protagonist. Like Hamilton as well, he recognizes that he can present at best an incomplete story, for Rimbaud's eleven years of self-willed exile have left comparatively few traces: letters to his family, some published reminiscences by colleagues, a handful of photographs. Nicholl aims to recreate not only the events and circumstances of Rimbaud's African sojourn, but also its sounds and smells. All the places Rimbaud knew, Nicholl gets to know—Charleville, London, Alexandria, Harar, Aden, Shoa—seeking to recapture a fleeting aura of this man who was absent even in presence. "I try to see him as they would have seen him," he muses during a visit to the Grand Hotel in Aden, where Rimbaud first set down his luggage. "He is really nothing special: a down-at-heel young Frenchman, a bit of a drifter. He is taciturn but seems nice enough."

Rimbaud is by nature a difficult subject. The "man with soles of wind," as his ex-lover Paul Verlaine tagged him, the man who wouldn't sit still for anyone, is no more accessible to his biographers than he was to the various family members, friends, or employers who tried to hold onto him. Nicholl is honest enough to recognize that, particularly for the mysterious period he has chosen to write about, factual traces will often have to join hands with educated guesswork, even pure speculation. To describe Rimbaud's arrival formalities on the docks of Aden, for instance, he at first dons his most self-assured tones to inform us that the poet "dislikes customs men: their pipes clenched between their teeth, their axes and knives, their dogs on the leash." And how does he come by such assurance? Quite simply, he doesn't, and by the next page he has taken down his all-knowing front, pulled back the curtain to reveal the jumble-box of disparate bits from which he has pieced together his tableau:

> My account owes something to a visit I made to Aden in 1991 . . . but mostly it derives from documentary sources. The bare facts can be gathered from one of Rimbaud's letters, and from the memoirs of the coffee trader Alfred Bardey . . . The surroundings are based on old photographs and descriptions of Aden [etc.] . . .
>
> It is not, of course, a definitive account: it is more like some scratchy old home-movie. The faces around him have blurred. There are jump-cuts due to lack of information. There are guesses . . .
>
> I do not really know that Rimbaud disliked customs men. One might suppose so from his poem "Customs Men," which according to his friend Delahaye recorded a run-in with the customs in Belgium, but a poem is not exactly an opinion, so this too is a guess.

Nor does he always accept these limitations with equanimity, for throughout *Somebody Else* runs a current of frustration, one no doubt familiar, though less baldly stated, to anyone attempting to recreate a lost moment in time. Walking through the boarded-up hulk of the Grand Hotel, he cannot help but reflect on the overwhelming sense of futility his mission elicits:

> Perhaps this was once Rimbaud's room. Who knows? Does it really matter if it was here, or somewhere down the corridor?

> Probably not. In coming to Aden I had hoped to find some clue to these "lost years" of Rimbaud's life, had hoped perhaps to find some moment of empathy . . . There are no ghosts here, no jolts of recognition, no physical traces. There may be a neatly carved "A.R. 1880" on some obscured wainscot, but I doubt it. This is just an old address.

The tone of pained regret, almost of spite, is our largest clue: Nicholl is viewing this place not like some thwarted scholar, but like an amnesiac desperately searching for pieces of his own identity. Throughout the book—and this is, at various moments, both its charm and its drawback—he shows an almost symbiotic involvement in the daily events of Rimbaud's African existence. He minutely charts the course of every failed get-rich-quick scheme Rimbaud dreamed up; lists, as Rimbaud did, every pound of coffee or bolt of cloth shipped to a client, every unit cost and profit calculation; worries over the weight-limit a mature camel could carry (200 kilos), the going rate for renting one (five thalers), the number of drivers, guides, and porters required for a given sales trip. He names and discusses every commodity Rimbaud traded in his eleven years, however briefly. His relation of the poet's unique stint as a gun runner—admittedly the most myth-laden episode of these years—alone covers six chapters.

There are times when he even indulges in affectionate spite, such as in this reflection on a dubious period description of Rimbaud's stay in an Abyssinian inn: "I cannot resist this untrustworthy memoir and the images it proffers. We are in this meagre little hotel on the Red Sea, circa September 1887. Rimbaud is in the dining room tucking into 'crab American-style'; Rimbaud is locked in his room in an aromatic cloud of Cairo hashish; Rimbaud is in the khazi with the shits from too much Abyssinian pepper."

Not only does Nicholl lead us through the minutiae of his research, sharing along the way musings on the joys and sorrows of obtaining it, but he also inserts himself into the narrative—not into Rimbaud's own history, of course (he leaves that to Edmund Morris), but into the backdrop against which it was played out. Naturally, most historians will visit the relevant sites; Nicholl, moreover, whose credits include several volumes of travel writing, is particularly adept at bringing Rimbaud's various surroundings to life, even when viewing them more than a century after the fact. Sometimes, however, Rimbaud's journey, and even Nicholl's work on it, get pushed aside by the author's own experience of these places. His presentation of Harar balances uneasily between necessary local color and personal reminiscence; his relation of an afternoon spent with an Amhara sex worker in Djibouti, while moving in its way, strikes one as pure self-indulgence. There is, in fact, an entire chapter on Djibouti, ostensibly prompted by Rimbaud's having stayed there en route to Shoa, in which the poet hardly appears at all, or like a very diffuse shadow against a background wall. Nicholl, on the other hand, does: here he is walking through the streets with camera in hand, being taunted by taxi drivers; here he is chewing *khat* with his Amhara friend, or dealing with beggars at a hotel terrace. Yes, these glimpses all add to our larger understanding of the context in which Arthur Rimbaud moved during this time. But they are also evidence of Charles Nicholl's desire—a desire in which he is by no means alone—to inch closer to the life of his subject, to establish, once again, that privileged relationship that acts as the motor of so many biographical endeavors.

Like Ian Hamilton, and to his credit, Nicholl comes clean about his personal reasons for undertaking this journey. In Hamilton's case, it was the individual message he'd read in *The Catcher in the Rye.* For Nicholl, as he tells us in an appendix, it had to do with one of those life-changing university friendships that some people are fortunate enough to have, with a fellow student named Kevin Stratford, who brought home to him the essence of what Rimbaud was, and whose death some years later might well have sparked Nicholl's biographical quest. "He was perhaps more Rimbaldian than any of the more obvious candidates among my acquaintance at that time," Nicholl writes in conclusion. "I still have the little Livre de Poche edition of Rimbaud he gave me, signing himself 'Le Bateleur,' the conjuror, a reference to the Tarot card of that ilk. It has accompanied me on my Rimbaud travels—to Charleville and Paris and Marseille, to Alexandria and Aden and Harar—and now, belatedly, I place this other book beside it in memory of Kevin and of those stringy teenage kids that we all once were. For 'belatedly,' of course, read 'too late.'"

*

"Too late": that is the hidden message of both these books, perhaps of all biographical obsessions. Too late to befriend Holden Caulfield, too late to accompany Rimbaud across the desert, too late to show Kevin the fruits of his influence. Too late, even when one does get to meet one's subject, to have known them "back then," as a potential equal (perhaps this is why memoirs about friendships with noteworthy figures, though useful, often have a distasteful air of smugness about them). All biography carries a distinct element of wishful thinking.

We see this best in a book that is not, strictly speaking, a biography at all. In 1988, the French novelist Patrick Modiano chanced upon a personal ad from a 1941 newspaper, asking for information about a missing Jewish teenager named Dora Bruder. The ad was placed in December, by her parents. In September of the following year, the names of both Dora and her father appeared on a list of Jewish deportees to Auschwitz. And between those two dates was nothing, a blank, that Modiano spent the next several years of his life trying to fill in. He eventually published his findings, and the story of his quest, in a beautifully spare and melancholy book titled, simply, *Dora Bruder.**

To discover who Dora was, what her life was like, and most of all, what she did in those months between disappearance and arrest, Modiano did what any creditable biographer would do: he revisited important neighborhoods, petitioned the authorities (often with great patience and ingenuity) for restricted documents, tracked down and interviewed survivors, pursued and discarded hypotheses, experienced his share of victories, obstacles, and dead ends. Like Hamilton and Nicholl, he shares (ostensibly) every step of his quest with the reader, sifting through obscure records and period accounts to try to recreate this otherwise unremarkable life, and in particular those few months that perhaps only Dora herself had ever known about.

What was it about this young girl's story that so absorbed him? It is true that much of Modiano's work, in both his novels and *Lacombe, Lucien* (1974), the screenplay he co-authored with Louis Malle, has wrestled with the situation of French Jews under the Occupation. It is true, as well, that he has a strong autobiographical attachment to the section of Paris in which Dora and her parents lived. "I've been familiar with the area around Boulevard Ornano [Dora's address] for a long time," he writes at the beginning. "When I was a child, I would go with my mother to the Saint-Ouen flea market . . . I was in that neighborhood in the winter of 1965. I had a girlfriend who lived on Rue Championne . . ." But most of all, Modiano's quest for Dora is closely bound to, and soon becomes intermingled with, his unresolved search

---

* Gallimard, 1997.

for his own Jewish father—a contemporary of Dora's who, like her, was arrested in a Gestapo dragnet, and who narrowly escaped a similar fate. In one scene, Modiano even imagines the two of them being carted off to headquarters in the same paddy wagon:

> I ended up convincing myself that it was in that glacial and lugubrious month of February [1942], when the special Police for Jewish Affairs set up dragnets in subway corridors, cinema entrances, and theater exits, that Dora had been caught . . . That same month of February, on the evening when the German regulations went into effect, my father had been picked up in a police roundup on the Champs-Elysées. Jewish Affairs inspectors had blocked the entrances and exits to a restaurant on Rue de Marignan where he was dining with a girlfriend. They had asked all the diners for their identity papers. My father didn't have any on him, and so they carted him off. In the paddy wagon taking him from the Champs-Elysées to Rue Greffulhe, headquarters of the Bureau of Jewish Affairs, he had noticed, amid the other shadows, a girl of about eighteen. He'd lost sight of her when they were made to walk upstairs, up to that police bureau and the office of its superintendent . . .
>
> He gave me no details about her face or clothing. I had almost forgotten about her, up until the day when I learned of Dora Bruder's existence. Then the presence of the girl in the paddy wagon with my father and other strangers, on that February night, resurfaced in my memory, and soon I began wondering if she hadn't been Dora Bruder, who had just been arrested as well before being sent to [the camp at] Tourelles.

But it wasn't Dora Bruder at all, as a list of the women interned at Tourelles later proves. "Maybe I wanted them to meet, my father and she, in that winter of 1942," Modiano finally admits, adding that if he "weren't here to write this," if Dora's story and his father's weren't made to coincide, at least momentarily, "no trace would remain of that unknown girl's presence, nor of my father's, in a paddy wagon on the Champs-Elysées in February 1942."

Not until shortly afterward, however, does the full emotional impact of this imagined coincidence become clear, when Modiano begins telling of another episode involving paddy wagons, and of his own arrest at the age of eighteen (the same age as Dora) some twenty years later:

> My parents were separated but lived in the same building, my father with a very high-strung woman who had straw-blonde hair. And I lived with my mother. A quarrel broke out between my parents on the landing that day, over the extremely modest stipend that the courts, after a lengthy battle, forced my father to pay for my support . . . My mother decided I'd have to go knock on his door and demand the money that he still hadn't paid. Unfortunately, we had nothing else to live on. I went very reluctantly. I rang his bell, intending to talk to him nicely, even to apologize for the whole thing. He slammed the door in my face. I heard the straw blonde screaming and calling the police, telling them a "hoodlum was causing a scene."

Picked up soon afterward, the young Modiano finds himself sitting in a police wagon opposite his father, who has come along to press charges. "While this was the first time in my life that such a thing happened, it occurred to me that my father had already experienced it twenty years before, that night in February 1942 . . . And I wondered if he too was thinking the same thing right then. But he pretended not to see me and avoided my eyes." At the police station, the young man is lectured by the superintendent and threatened with jail time as his father watches impassively, but finally is let off with a warning. Modiano continues:

> We left the station, my father and I. I asked if it had really been necessary to call the police and "charge" me in front of those officers. He didn't answer. I didn't hold it against him. Since we lived in the same building, we walked our common way, side by side, in silence. I almost brought up the night of February 1942 when they had also thrown him into a paddy wagon, to ask if he'd thought about it a little while back. But perhaps it didn't matter as much to him as it did to me.
>
> We didn't exchange a single word during our entire walk, nor in the stairwell before parting company. I would see him two or three times more the following year, in August, when he stole my military papers in an attempt to have me drafted into the Reuilly barracks. After that I never saw him again.

Dora Bruder is a book imbued with the spirit of loss, in which every search, every inquiry comes too late. Even though Modiano saves Dora from anonymity, he comes too late to help her. He is too late to make amends with his father, or (as he notes at one point) to "respond to all those people"—officials, police, the antisemitic writers his father studied, the black marketeers and French Gestapo officials he consorted with—"whose insults had wounded me through my father." And when the elder Modiano lies in a hospital, years after their last contact, his son arrives too late to find the deathbed.

In its way, *Dora Bruder* is perhaps the purest example of autobiographical biography. As with the two books discussed above, the story of Modiano's subject is tightly bound to the story of his research. The book could stand as a model case study of the biographer's craft and motivations, all the more so in that Dora herself, if the truth be told, is exemplary neither as an historical figure nor as a Jew who was murdered under the Occupation. Dora's main importance for Modiano lies in the parallels that he draws between her, his lost, insufficiently lamented father, and finally himself. For him, the real tragedy lies in the fact that, however arduous his quest, his father will remain lost, and Dora will remain a mystery. Modiano's closing paragraph harbors a lesson that any biographer, thinking to penetrate and explicate the soul of another human being, would do well to ponder:

> I will never know how she spent her days, where she hid, whose company she kept during those winter months the first time she ran away, and over those few weeks in the spring when she ran away again. That is her secret. A poor and precious secret that executioners, regulations, so-called Occupation authorities, the city jail, barracks, camps, history, time—everything that sullies and destroys you—could not steal from her.

⋆

Biography is not a process of direct identification. One does not have to be infatuated with a literary figure (or actor turned politician) to write one. At the same time, to undergo the years of research, rebuffs, and revisions implies something more intimate than simple curiosity, or the lure of a publisher's advance. Can those years really be compensated by the minor fame garnered in usually restricted circles, or the brief shower of reviews, or the fee that often wouldn't cover the annual salary of the editor's assistant? Can those inducements explain entire days spent fretting over someone else's exact height and shoe size, what she ate for lunch on a given day?

To be sure, there is a legitimate value to the restoration of lived history, which is central to any biography worthy of the label. But the motives are rarely so pure as we, toilers in the groves, would like to pretend. For those whose cool objectivity is sometimes tinctured with sweat, blood, and bile, there is another, more essential component: a questing for oneself, sought in glimpses and fleeting points of contact between one's self-image and the actions and traits of someone who, in reality, probably has very little in common with his or her dogged interpreter. When I set out to write the life of André Breton, I was, of course, intrigued by the great public stands, the adventure that was Surrealism, the explorations and friendships that characterized his long run on the intellectual stage. But what kept me attached for nearly ten years, what held me in that front-row seat night after night as Breton played out his operatic dramas, were smaller details, the ones that showed me that here was a man who asked some of the same questions, held some of the same aspirations, and—alas—made some of the same mistakes as I had. The details, in other words, that can foster the insane but pervasive illusion that we have entered into a unique understanding with someone never met and perhaps long dead, an understanding that (we are convinced) even the subject's closest friends and loved ones couldn't share—and how dare those friends and loved ones, not to mention the subject himself (as in Ian Hamilton's case), object when we presume to manhandle the intimate detritus of his life! And even more so when we then undertake to render our findings public, effectively bragging to all the world, with however much humility or respect, that we and we alone were granted this privileged audience.

Given half a chance, a biographer (and I do not exempt myself from this) will wax expansive about the particular hardships and satisfactions of the craft: one always wants an opportunity to air one's war stories. But what these efforts mask—and when the story of the writing becomes part of the writing itself, that mask can wear disturbingly thin—is a love-hate dialogue with an often unwitting interlocutor; a fascination with certain aspects of the other's actions or character, coupled with a kind of resentment, even revulsion, against that same person for having made us feel so attracted in the first place.

We might as well be honest with ourselves: at its core, and stripped of its patina of scholarly respectability, the researcher's m. o. and impetus are not so very different from the stalker's, with some of the same hunger for information and recognition, the same dark wish to enter into and subsume the other's existence and accomplishments, the other's notoriety. Don't we know it, deep down. And don't they know it, too, those widows and executors and former comrades-in-arms who spurn our earnest advances, our requests for what is at bottom a 500-page autograph. When all is said and done, the ultimate biographer might well be, not Richard Ellmann or Robert Caro, but Mark David Chapman.

ART OF THE INANE

To anyone who has read Flaubert, it will come as no surprise that optimism was not his strong suit. Especially on the topic of human nature and its foibles, he always seemed ready to believe the worst. The roots of his despairing and disparaging view stretch way deep: already at the tender age of nine, young Gustave was telling a friend, "If you'd like us to work together at writing, I'll write comedies and you can write your dreams. And since there's a lady who comes to see papa and always says stupid things, I'll write them too." Later, when barely in his teens, he and his pals devised a fictitious persona, "Le Garçon" ("the Boy"), a kind of anarchic yokel whom they took turns play-acting in order to mouth utter inanities to unsuspecting victims, while those in on the joke laughed themselves silly.

As an adult, Flaubert never lost his fascination with, and loathing for, human idiocy, using it instead as the driving force behind much of his writing. His most celebrated novel, *Madame Bovary*, is built around the ruinous gap between the romantic clichés filling Emma Bovary's head and the cold, sad reality of what happens when her dreams more or less come true. And *Sentimental Education*, perhaps his darkest book, is a ruthlessly cynical look at unrequited passion and the unrealizable dreams of its protagonist, Frédéric Moreau.

It was not just the foibles of others that fueled Flaubert's creativity. Firmly in the sights of his ironic skepticism were his own shortcomings as well, dissected with a surgeon's precision and dispassion, or—perhaps more appropriately for this former law student—a jurist's fine attention to damning detail: Madame Bovary was, after all, *"moi"*; and in *Sentimental Education*, the young Moreau, arriving in Paris with a headful of half-baked ambitions, shares more than a few traits with his creator—not least among them Moreau's unfulfilled and slightly ridiculous passion for a beguiling older woman named Mme. Arnoux, based on Flaubert's own long and unrequited infatuation with the vivacious Parisian socialite Elisa Schlesinger.

But nowhere does asininity, in all its facets, take center stage as much as in Flaubert's last, unfinished novel, *Bouvard and Pécuchet.* A compendium of the clichés and received wisdom that held sway in the author's time, told through the misadventures of two clueless nincompoops who seem remarkable only in the grandiosity of their failures, *Bouvard and Pécuchet* would seem to be the novel Flaubert had been preparing to write all his life. And indeed, insofar as it distills his abiding dismay at human folly, the book's genesis can be traced to well before he first set quill to paper on it in 1874, at the age of fifty-two. Reflections on the subject dot his letters to various friends and intimates over a period of decades. To his lover Louise Colet, around 1852: "Saint Polycarp used to stuff up his ears, flee from wherever he was, and cry: 'In what times, O Lord, hast thou caused me to be born!' I am becoming like Saint Polycarp." To his close friend, the novelist George Sand, in 1867: "Stupidity and injustice make me roar. And in my corner I grumble against many things that are 'none of my business.'" To the Russian novelist Ivan Turgenev, in 1872: "Never have things of the mind counted for less. Never have hatred of all greatness, scorn of Beauty, and execration of literature been so outspoken." One could go on, and on.

It was in that same year, 1872, that Flaubert first announced his plan to write a novel "in which I'll vent all my anger," as he told the literary salonist Edma des Genettes. "Yes, at last I shall rid myself of what is stifling me. I shall vomit back onto my contemporaries the disgust they inspire in me, even if it means ripping my chest open." As it happened, the announcement was premature, and it was not until two years later that he wrote to Turgenev: "On Saturday, August 1, I shall at last begin *Bouvard and Pécuchet*! There will be no turning back. But such terror! It is as though I were embarking on an immensely long voyage, toward unknown regions, and that I shall never return." In fact, he never did return, for in 1880, six years into the writing, he died suddenly of a cerebral hemorrhage, still two chapters away from the end of his voyage.

That said, the ten sections he did finish are as crystalline and polished as anything Flaubert ever wrote, for his practice was to refine each chapter to perfection—or as close as he could get—before moving on to the next, and even then only grudgingly. "Each time I read it over, I discover new flaws! It has to be *perfect*," he complained to his niece after completing one of the last chapters. Moreover, thanks to his detailed notes, we also have an excellent idea of how the story was to end. These notes not only provide a schematic conclusion to the novel, but also give us a privileged glimpse into the author's working method, as if he were inviting us backstage to see the scaffolding.

Why did Flaubert decide to begin writing *Bouvard and Pécuchet* when he did? We can pinpoint several reasons, but among the most significant is that in April 1872, shortly before he first announced his plan to write the book, Flaubert's cherished mother, with whom he had lived most of his adult life, succumbed to a prolonged illness. "I have realized during the past fortnight that my poor dear mother was the human being I loved the most. It's as though a part of my entrails were torn away," he wrote to George Sand. At the same time, the passing seems to have acted as a kind of liberation, a removal of constraints: "I shall at last vent my resentment, vomit my hatred, spit out my bile, ejaculate my rage, purge my indignation," he told his friend Léonie Brainne that summer, in terms remarkably similar to the ones he used with Edma des Genettes.

And Flaubert had plenty of resentment to vent. Fifteen years earlier, the widely-publicized obscenity trial over *Madame Bovary*, though ultimately resolved in the author's favor, had demoralized him to the point of wishing "to return, once and for all, to the solitude and the silence from which I emerged; I should like to publish nothing, and never again have myself talked about." It's true that in those fifteen years, he wrote and published the lengthy novels *Salammbo* and *Sentimental Education* and rewrote *The Temptation of Saint Anthony*, but regardless: the trial still stung. More recently, the Franco-Prussian War of 1870 and the civil revolts that followed, during which Flaubert served as a local drill sergeant, had left him "nauseated, heartbroken at the stupidity of [his] fellow countrymen [and] the incorrigible barbarism of the human race." Not surprisingly, these experiences were caricatured soon afterward in *Bouvard and Pécuchet*, under the guise of the Revolution of 1848. And in 1875, even as he was engaged in writing the book, the financial ruin of his beloved niece Caroline led him to spend nearly all his savings in an attempt to rescue her and her husband, condemning him to what he termed a "permanent state of uncertainty." Overall, the blackness that suffuses this comedy from start to finish, and that deepens as the story nears what would have been its end, largely reflects Flaubert's own state of mind in his twilight years.

⋆

Bouvard and Pécuchet tells the story of two copy clerks, François Denys Bouvard and Juste Romain Pécuchet, who meet at the beginning of the novel and become fast friends. This is the first comic touch, for these two are about as odd a couple as you could ever hope to find: Bouvard is corpulent, lusty, exuberant, fond of wine, women, and song; Pécuchet is ascetic, parsimonious, cautious to a fault, and seemingly fond of nothing. Despite this, their shared profession as copyists, and a certain mutual simpatico that seems to transcend the differences, bring them together. When Bouvard unexpectedly inherits a small fortune from a long-lost relative, the two decide to leave Paris and their jobs and buy a farm in Normandy. And there the headaches begin.

The trouble is that these two inveterate city dwellers, heretofore confirmed singletons living in furnished apartments, know nothing about small town life, farming, home ownership, do-it-yourselfism, or, perhaps most disastrously of all, how to deal with people. Nevertheless, convinced of their own abilities—even of a certain untapped genius—they immediately set about restoring their ramshackle farm according to the most grandiose plans and try to turn it into a major agricultural concern, all the while fancying themselves local notables among the resident bourgeoisie. When each of their attempts goes spectacularly wrong, they move on to other pursuits, including, over the course of the novel, chemistry and medicine, history and archeology, literature and aesthetics, politics and government, love and romance, spiritualism and religion, athletics and pedagogy—in other words, all the great fields of human endeavor as European culture understood them at the time, each one approached by our two heroes with a bullish faith in their own innate talents that more or less guarantees disaster.

Like their creator, and in keeping with their former profession of copy clerks, Bouvard and Pécuchet seek to learn not so much by doing as by reading, with each new undertaking bringing a fresh load of books into the house. And each new bout of literature only confirms the disheartening fact that, for every foolproof theory or unassailable approach, there are ten other, equally foolproof theories to contradict it, cloud the issue, and confuse our hapless autodidacts to the point of desperation. The most common refrain in the novel is, "They gave up."

The real calamity, of course, is not that Bouvard and Pécuchet get flummoxed by all these competing theories and dubious pronouncements, but that they then go forth, time after time after time, to put their foggy notions of what they've only dimly understood into practice. A typical passage from early in the book describes what happens when the would-be entrepreneurs, having soured on the idea of becoming gentleman farmers, decide instead to try their hand at creating luxury preserves and fine liqueurs:

> Fourteen jars were filled with peas and tomatoes. They sealed the lids with quicklime and cheese, applied strips of cloth around the rims, then plunged them into boiling water. It evaporated. They poured in cold water; the difference in temperature shattered the jars. Only three were saved.
>
> Then they bought old sardine tins, stuffed them with veal cutlets, and plunged them into a double boiler. They came out round as balloons; they would flatten once they cooled off. To pursue the experiment, they stuffed other tins with eggs, chicory, lobster, fish stew, and some soup. And they congratulated themselves, like Mr. Appert, on having "preserved the seasons." According to Pécuchet, such discoveries were more worthy than the exploits of the conquerors . . .
>
> They purchased the holdings of a bankrupt distiller, and their house soon saw the arrival of sieves, casks, funnels, skimmers, straining bags, and scales, not to mention a crushing bowl with a metal ball and a Moorshead still, which required a reflector furnace with a ventilation hood . . .
>
> Finally, they dreamed of a cream liqueur that would outshine all the others. They would use coriander as in kummel, kirsch as in maraschino, hyssop as in chartreuse, ambrette as in

Vespetro, *Calamus aromaticus* as in Krambambuli, and they would color it red with sandalwood. But what name should they market it under? For they needed a label that would be easy to remember, yet still exotic. Having considered many possibilities, they settled on "Bouvarine" . . .

When the ingredients for "Bouvarine" had finally been assembled, they stuffed them all into the cucurbit along with some alcohol, lit the fire, and waited. Meanwhile, Pécuchet took the tins from the armoire. He opened the lid of the first, then a second, then a third. He tossed them aside in a rage and called Bouvard over.

Bouvard shut the spout of the coil and hurried toward the preserves. Their disappointment was complete. The slices of veal looked like boiled shoe soles. A murky liquid had replaced the lobster. The fish stew was beyond recognition. Mushrooms were growing on the soup. And the entire laboratory reeked with an intolerable stench.

Suddenly, with the sound of a grenade, the still exploded in twenty pieces that flew as high as the ceiling, puncturing the pots, flattening the skimmers, shattering the glassware. The coal scattered in all directions, the oven was a wreck, and the next day Germaine found a spatula in the barnyard.

The pressure from the steam had blown the instrument apart, especially since the head of the cucurbit had been shut.

Pécuchet had immediately ducked behind the vat and Bouvard had flattened on a stool. For ten solid minutes they remained that way, not daring to make the slightest move, pale with terror, in the midst of the glass shards. When they were again able to speak, they wondered what could be the cause of so many misfortunes, and especially this latest one? And they didn't understand a thing, except that they had narrowly escaped death.

You might reasonably suspect that after a while, this constant cycle of attempt and failure—new attempt and new failure—further attempt and further failure—might become rather tedious. If so, you are no different from Flaubert himself, who, even while confessing to Mme. Brainne that his "secret goal" with this book was "to so dumbfound the reader that he goes mad," predicted that he would not succeed "for the simple reason that the reader won't read me—the book will put him to sleep from the start." And to Emile Zola he lamented, "There are no quotable *excerpts*, no brilliant scenes, just the same situation over and over . . . I'm scared it might bore people to death." This was not an unreasonable fear. Even as the novel was being written, one prominent critic complained to the same Zola that "you see two snails trying to climb Mont Blanc. The first time they fall is amusing; the tenth is unbearable"—and many other reviewers echoed the same complaint after the book's publication in 1881, the year after its author's death.

Unappreciated it was, but boring it is not, once we've accepted the ground rules. And though the book adopts from early on a notably repetitive structure and conceit, a kind of hilariously low-key non-plot, we might even pinpoint that very repetitiveness as a huge part of its comic effect. Think of the Three Stooges' head bonks and nose tweaks, or Laurel and Hardy's fine messes: the more we expect them, the funnier they become.

But more to the point, while the reiterated buffoonery of *Bouvard and Pécuchet* provides a reliable comic leitmotif, the book is much more than a record of two snails climbing Mont Blanc. It is also about more than simple self-delusion, or lampooning moronic social policies and intellectual fashions. Underlying and paralleling all of these are several grander themes that lift the novel above mere opera buffa.

On the one hand, *Bouvard and Pécuchet* is a classic tale of human aspiration: the age-old desire to be more than oneself, to reach fulfillment, to find happiness. Products of a time and culture that believed staunchly in the beneficence of scientific progress and the imperatives of conformity, Flaubert's protagonists struggle to come to terms with the onslaught of new knowledge confronting them, and with the societal attitudes that accompany it, by living out a veritable encyclopedia of modern pursuits. Pushed by their mutual shame at the limits of their education, as well as by their shared hunger for public recognition, they set out to master discipline after discipline at an impossibly accelerated rate. The fact that they are so hopelessly inept furnishes the laughs; but it should not obscure the fact that their striving, in itself, is among humanity's nobler attributes.

In addition, this is the story of a remarkable friendship. Friendship is the emotional anchor that gives the novel true depth, the kernel around which its moments of genuine pathos crystallize. The fact is, for all his curmudgeonliness vis-à-vis his fellows, in his own life Flaubert invested a huge amount of emotional energy in close platonic friendships with a few intimates, male and female. Two men in particular, Alfred Le Poittevin and Louis Bouilhet, both dead by the time he began writing *Bouvard and Pécuchet*, had been very dear comrades, and these attachments no doubt served him in sketching the portrait of his two protagonists and their sometimes kvetchy but ultimately unshakable bond.

Flaubert's love life was, on the other hand, not the most straightforward. A devotee of prostitutes, hermitic by nature, he does not seem to have pursued women with great conviction. His decidedly lukewarm interest in hearth, home, and female companionship can be glimpsed in this retort to the maternally solicitous George Sand, who had made the mistake of broaching the subject with him: "As for sharing my life with a woman—marrying, as you advise—I find the prospect fantastic," he admonished. "Woman has never fitted into my existence." In *Bouvard and Pécuchet*, the character of Mme. Bordin, with whom Bouvard conducts a desultory courtship, no doubt reflects Flaubert's on-again, off-again affair with his sometime lover Louise Colet.

There is yet another aspect of the novel that stands out, and that is the authorial stance—or rather, its lack. When *Bouvard and Pécuchet* was begun, memories were still fresh of France's humiliating defeat at the hands of the Prussian army in 1870, and of the bloody repression of the radical Paris Commune in 1871 and the civil hatreds it stirred. In some ways, this period mirrored the earlier Revolution of 1848, which had begun as a revolt against the monarchy but ended with the establishment of the conservative Second Empire. In both cases, the headiness of revolutionary ideals had ultimately led only to more repression and mind-numbing conformity. Many authors of the preceding generation, such as George Sand, had believed in, and militated for, the radicalist ideals of '48; for them, those ideals were still valid and still quickened the blood, even if ultimately they had come to naught, and their writings reflected their sympathies. Flaubert, on the other hand, looked upon these ideals with profound skepticism; for him, the bombastic pronouncements emitted by both sides, along with the self-serving egotism that always seemed to pump up these conflicting ideologies, were a joke at best, a tragedy at worst. As he wrote to Sand in 1871, from a Paris still reeling from the aftermath of the Commune: "The sight of the ruins is nothing compared to the great Parisian insanity. With very rare exceptions, everybody seemed to me only fit for the strait-jacket. One half of the population longs to hang the other half, which returns the compliment." The fact that *Bouvard and Pécuchet* is set in the 1840s allows Flaubert to telescope France's two recent political upheavals, using one to lampoon the other, while standing aloof from any allegiance.

Little wonder that the cynicism of *Sentimental Education* and the equal-opportunity mockery of *Bouvard and Pécuchet* so distressed the normally supportive Sand, who deplored the younger Flaubert's pessimism and urged him to show some indulgence toward her generation's lost illusions, in tones not unlike those of an ex-hippie urging a smirking Gen-X teen not to knock the tie-dye. Flaubert responded with what amounts to a miniature aesthetic credo: "I assure you that I do not paint the world in 'desolate colors' for my own pleasure; after all, I cannot change my eyes. As for my 'lack of convictions,' alas! I am only too full of convictions. I burst with suppressed anger and indignation. But my ideal of Art demands that the artist show none of this, and that he appear in his work no more than God in nature. The man is nothing, the work is everything!" It is this refusal to fall into partisanship for either point of view, the jaundiced eye the novel casts on dogma of all hues, that remains one of its most modern—not to say postmodern—attributes.

Misunderstood in its time, *Bouvard and Pécuchet* has since come to be recognized as Flaubert's most groundbreaking book, a precursor to and cornerstone of modernist literature, as well as one of the great comic masterpieces of the nineteenth century (or for that matter, of any century). It is modern not only in its attitudes, but also, perhaps even more so, in its use of language, of the stuff of writing itself. For along with the zeitgeist he deplored, what Flaubert challenges in *Bouvard and Pécuchet* are the accepted conventions of storytelling. Structural conventions, which dictate that the hero's adventures be varied enough to maintain the reader's interest—whereas here, each chapter follows its stubbornly uniform path, its more or less unvarying series of catastrophes. Psychological conventions, which require the protagonist to undergo some form of evolution—whereas Bouvard and Pécuchet emerge at the other end of their long journey remarkably similar to where they started. And perhaps most of all, fictional conventions, which insist that the characters and their actions stay within the frame of their narrative—whereas here, with the seemingly endless parade of authorities cited as an integral part of the story, the novel effectively overspills its own composition.

To amplify that last point: even as he was writing *Bouvard and Pécuchet*, Flaubert was compiling a lexicon of numbskullery, much of it culled from the 1500 books he read as background research, and much of which he found hopelessly inane. He eventually titled this lexicon the "Dictionary of Accepted Ideas," and it is so central to his project that it is often included as an appendix to *Bouvard and Pécuchet*. The dictionary functions as a kind of parallel text to the novel, the Cliffs-Notes version of the two men's bumbling quest for instant knowledge. It acts as a compressed record of the source materials Flaubert himself plowed through as he read up on the various subjects his protagonists tackle—that is, as he grappled in real time with the same source materials that his characters consult in the novel. A mere few entries can give a taste of his daily diet for the six years of the book's composition, their prescriptions for life dispensed like fortune cookie wisdom:

> ABSINTHE: Ultra-violent poison: one glass and you're dead.
> BANDITS: Always fierce.
> ILLEGIBLE: What a doctor's prescription should be. Same for signatures: this shows that one is inundated with correspondence.
> ILLUSIONS: Claim to have many. Lament having lost them.
> LITERATURE: The occupation of idle people.

and so on, for a good two dozen pages.

Even the book's ending highlights the permeability, the interchangeability of the writing and reading experiences. Practically the last sentence, in the notes to what would have been its final chapter, goes: "They [Bouvard and Pécuchet] recapitulate their actions and thoughts, which for the reader should be a critique of the novel." It's a tantalizing, serpent's-tail ending that reinforces just how much, in this book, the medium is indeed the message.

It is in this regard, as well as in its celebration of the *everydayness* of everyday life, that *Bouvard and Pécuchet* anticipates the modernist mainstays of the twentieth century, from the novels of Joyce and Musil down to films like Jim Jarmusch's *Stranger than Paradise* and TV shows like *Seinfeld*, passing via such figures as Borges, Calvino, Perec, and the New Novelists. *Bouvard and Pécuchet* is not Flaubert's most famous book, and it is hardly the first to critique an author's times and society. But in its ability to create the *illusion* of humdrum life (and keep it engaging), its self-devouring structure, and its humor that progressively corrodes the reader's every acquired certainty, it might well be the most forward-looking novel of the nineteenth century.

SURREALISM'S CHILDREN

Back when I was an idealistic young soul, I enrolled in a PhD program in French and Comparative Literature, intent on making a career in academia. Those were the days when New Criticism and Semiotics held sway, and texts were to be read without interference from outside influences. The approach we were taught, boiled down, was that all a reader needed to know about a poem or a work of prose could be found on the page, without reference to historical context, authorial biography, or any other distractions. In class after class, we dissected poems by Ronsard and Rimbaud, the Symbolists and the Surrealists, peeling back layer upon layer of manifest and latent content. It was intoxicating stuff, but I couldn't escape a nagging question: What was the point of it? Wasn't literature supposed to tell us about more than just its own internal machinery? What did all this have to do with, you know, life? Unable to resolve these questions, I handed in my Master's thesis and said goodbye to all that.

One effect of having left academia prematurely is that I spent the following decades still grappling with the appropriate balance between art and life, and the role that literature, literary studies, and the humanities in general have to play in our dealings with this fraught and confusing world—a world that, increasingly, seems resistant to the kinds of challenges and provocations that art and literature are best suited to pose. Is literature meant to reinforce our convictions, or to destabilize them? Should art be a safe space or a dangerous one, and what does that mean? What is the role of the off-putting, the upsetting, the offensive, and the shocking in our study and consumption of the humanities? Can art still *be* shocking in this day and age? And who, exactly, is being shocked?

The answers used to be fairly straightforward, or so it seemed. The progressive avant-garde duly épaté'd the bourgeois, who duly responded with howls of outrage as their cherished shibboleths—God, king, country, the army, the Establishment, what have you—were dragged through the slime, often in language and aesthetic forms that were themselves a provocation. Provocation was even a kind of social role, an expected feature of the societal landscape. But things are no longer so simple.

These days we find ourselves in a situation in which supposedly contradictory viewpoints circle each other, ouroboros-like, and become virtually impossible to distinguish. Conservatives vent their offense by banning an increasing number of books in schools and libraries, while college professors are actively discouraged from teaching material that might ruffle student sensibilities and provost's offices disinvite speakers deemed too hot to handle. Yet what better time than in college to have sensibilities ruffled? When will students ever have a more free and insulated space in which to rub shoulders with controversial ideas, and to develop the skills needed to confront those ideas in the world—that is, to view them with greater insight and deeper understanding, if only to then refute them? College is, or should be, an instruction in controversy and its skills. For this reason, the curricular exclusions on today's campuses not only curtail what the educational experience has to offer, but, particularly in a study of the humanities, the erecting of such guardrails undermines what is most valuable about the discipline: its challenge to comfort and certainty, its impetus to make us think harder and more independently.

We are all familiar with the Golden Age of Bourgeois Indignation, in incidents ranging from theatergoers howling at the premiere of Victor Hugo's *Hernani* in 1830, to attendees at the Paris Salon in 1863 trying to slash Manet's *Déjeuner sur l'herbe*, to audiences throwing tomatoes and raw steaks at Dada performers in the 1920s. Flash forward a century and the dynamic has reversed: as Laura Kipnis has observed in her essay "Transgression, an Elegy," it's not the rubes and the philistines who get rattled now, but rather the progressives and the illuminati who find it hard to stomach the provocations. "At some point," she writes, "offendability moved its offices to the hip side of town." Nor, even, is outrage the exclusive privilege of the avant-garde. In the current climate, mainstream art and literature can just as likely get dinged as the cutting-edge stuff, in a free-for-all of offense.

The question is, what do we sacrifice by avoiding such offense? It's not always pleasant to be rattled out of one's complacencies—the entire history of the avant-garde banked on it—but in losing the displeasure of injury, are we also losing the pleasures of discovery, and of self-discovery, that can accompany it? The price of comfort is often stagnation.

And there's a more immediate concern as well: in this time of anonymous reputation-bashing and swift retaliation against unwelcome opinion—the so-called "cancel culture"—the danger is not so much that people's ratings will suffer and their speaking engagements will be revoked, but that they will stop saying anything at all for fear of being boycotted or "shamed." We have too many crises to confront, none of which can be meaningfully addressed in pre-approved 280-character soundbites, for those who can see beyond partisanship to refrain from making valid contributions. Trying to avoid offense in every instance is a fool's errand—you can't please all of the people all of the time—and holding back consequential and constructive insights, even if unpopular, impedes the free exchange of ideas and accomplishes nothing.*

---

* It seems superfluous to add that the situation has changed drastically since 2022, when this essay was written. In a period of punitive and lawless retaliation against viewpoints deemed "un-American" (i.e., those that don't flatter the current regime), the danger is not so much being boycotted as detained or deported. Nonetheless, I persist in feeling that the main point remains valid: there is too much

★

From its tumultuous start, the Surrealist movement was out to shock. The flurry of activity that accompanied its debut in late 1924 and early 1925, including the broadside *A Corpse* (which spat on the much beloved and recently deceased novelist Anatole France, an act of cultural blasphemy), the aggressive prose and propositions of André Breton's *Manifesto of Surrealism* ("Beloved imagination, what I most like in you is your unsparing quality"), and the common cause that the group tried to make with the reviled Communist Party, were not only steps toward defining a philosophical program, but also ways of slapping bourgeois proprieties repeatedly across the face.

This was true of both their actions and their proclaimed choice of role models, many of whom would not have passed a modern-day ethics test. The most glaring case in point is the Marquis de Sade, poster boy for aberrant sexuality and one of Surrealism's lauded heroes. (Many more examples can be found in Breton's *Anthology of Black Humor*, a veritable rogue's gallery of dubious precursors.) Sade's novels are jampacked with physical and mental abuse, coprophagia, cannibalism, torture, rape, and murder perpetrated indiscriminately against women and men of all ages: he did not lend his name to a major psychopathology lightly. Nor were these acts merely theoretical, for the man practiced what he predicated—not to the extent portrayed in his books, not by a long shot, but enough to keep him behind bars for nearly half his

---

at stake for those with reasoned, informed critiques to keep silent. And there is too much at stake for any of us, regardless of our political or moral persuasion, to shy away from engaging with perspectives not our own, if only to counter them meaningfully. (*Note from 2025.*)

seventy-four years, first under the monarchy, then under the French Revolution, then again under Napoleon. And we must be clear: Sade was no innocent victim. He used his wealth and his privilege to indulge in prodigious sexual predation, like an eighteenth-century Jeffrey Epstein. As such, his life and his books have been a thorn in the side of progressive-minded thinkers for the past two centuries. How can you promote freedom of expression and still defend *that*?

And yet his work has been defended, and persuasively so, by such formidable intellectuals as Angela Carter, Roland Barthes, Maurice Blanchot (whose monograph *Lautréamont and Sade* owes much to Surrealist thinking), Susan Sontag, and Michel Foucault, to name just a few. Why would they do this? One answer comes from Simone de Beauvoir, in her landmark analysis of Sade's writings from 1953, titled, appropriately, "Must We Burn Sade?" Sade, she declared, "drained to the dregs the moment of selfishness, injustice, and misery, and he insisted upon its truth. The supreme value of his testimony is the fact that it disturbs us. It forces us to reexamine thoroughly the basic problem which haunts our age in different forms: the true relation between man and man." In a rare moment of convergence between De Beauvoir and the Surrealists, the poet Paul Eluard anticipated this view in 1937 in his book *L'Evidence poétique*, writing: "Sade wanted to restore to civilized man the power of his primitive instincts . . . He believed that out of this, and this alone, true equality would come. Since virtue is its own reward, he labored, in the name of everything that suffers, to drag it down and humiliate it . . . with no illusions and no lies, so that those it normally condemns might build here on earth a world on the immense scale of mankind."

The arguments for and against Sade are many and complex, and they are also largely familiar. On one side, De Beauvoir defends him as a cold-eyed realist. On the other, writers such as Andrea Dworkin warn that his books, like any form of pornography, could incite acts of violence, especially against women. Both arguments have validity, and it is not a cop-out to admit that there is no single answer. If anything, the true energy of art and literature might reside in the questions they pose rather than the certainties they offer. What I will say is that, more than the events portrayed in his books, which are so over-the-top that they often become plainly absurd, perhaps the most shocking thing about reading Sade is how *un*-titillating so much of it is. As you plow though description upon minute description of various improbable scenarios, their inflexible regulation ultimately undermines any eroticism they might have been meant to contain. Ironically, the parts of Sade's work for which he is the most infamous are actually the most tedious.

The intriguing part, to pick up from De Beauvoir, is Sade's lucidity. Interspersed with the horrific actions are many pages of philosophy—I would go so far as to call it moral philosophy—that take an unsparing and unflinching view of human interactions, and strip away the pieties with which we have comforted ourselves for two millennia. Here, for instance, is one of Sade's fictional stand-ins instructing an eager young pupil about vice and virtue:

> Nature has endowed each of us with a capacity for kindly feelings: let us not squander them on others . . . Let us feel when it is to [our] advantage; and when it is not, let us be absolutely unbending. From this exact economy of feeling, from this judicious use of sensibility, there results a kind of cruelty which is sometimes not without its delights. One cannot always do evil; deprived of the pleasure if affords, we can at least find the sensation's equivalent in the minor but piquant wickedness of never doing good.

Nietzsche is not far away.

It is worth recalling that what landed Sade in the Bastille was not so much his acts of cruelty as the fact that he had sex with both men and women, and perhaps even more so that he was accused (though never convicted) of blasphemy against the highly influential and politically connected Church, which did not countenance challenges to its celestial worldview or its sovereignty. It is also worth remembering that his books (such as the above-quoted *Philosophy in the Bedroom*) were written during the long years he spent in various prisons and asylums, and that in many ways their vindictive savagery—their sadism, if you will—can be read as a howl of rage against captivity, no matter which political regime was in charge. It is again De Beauvoir who notes that "Sade does not give us the work of a free man. He makes us participate in his efforts at liberation. But it is precisely for this reason that he holds our attention." The value of a figure such as Sade, in other words, lies not in the acts that he describes but in the ethical challenges that he poses. It is one thing to create from a position of moral good, as many great writers and artists have done. But a steady diet of such work gives you only half the story, and not always the more necessary half.

So the question remains: Is Sade worth reading on these grounds, or should he indeed be burned? Is the offense that his writings constitute a reason for locking his work away, as he himself was locked away—and as his manuscripts were locked away for decades in the so-called "Hell" section of the French National Library? Or do his "efforts at liberation," or his decidedly unsentimental views on society, offer reasons to look beyond the parts we find distasteful? Is the threat posed by Sade that his books beget actual horrors, as Dworkin argued? Or that, long before Freud came along, they upended our complacent belief in the basic altruism of people and forced us to observe human nature at its ugliest and most unnerving?

These questions are all the more relevant in that, unlike so many of his contemporaries, Sade's impact did not fade with time. In 1959, the Canadian conceptual artist Jean Benoît, under the auspices of the Surrealist group, performed a piece called *The Execution of the Testament of the Marquis de Sade*. Benoît was well aware that his invitation-only audience would not be easy to impress: gathered that evening in the commodious Paris apartment of the poet Joyce Mansour were some one hundred "writers, poets, painters, filmmakers, critics . . . women in evening gowns . . . their nails painted blue or green . . . As well as a woman in black velvet whose nipple fit through a small hole in her dress." At a prearranged signal, the attendees stood in a semicircle facing a stage area, their ears assaulted by the recorded sounds of an erupting volcano and readings from Sade's works. Benoît then appeared, dressed in an ornate black costume with spikey protrusions over his chest and legs, a grotesquely extended erection, and a cape from which blood seemed to be dripping. Piece by piece his costume was slowly removed by his wife, the artist Mimi Parent, revealing his nude body to be painted all in black, his heart covered by a red star (Sade's emblem). With a shrill cry, Benoît grabbed a red-hot iron placed nearby and branded the word "Sade" into his flesh, squarely over his heart. He then held out the still-smoking iron to his audience and demanded, "Who's next?" The Chilean painter Roberto Matta was so carried away by the performance that he spontaneously rushed up, tore open his shirt, and seared his own left breast.

Benoît's performance marks a relatively anomalous point on the timeline of outrage that I alluded to above, in that the members of the audience were clearly rattled—in Matta's case, to the point of voluntarily broiling his own flesh—but they were not offended. They had come in search of provocation, and they were not disappointed. How that performance might fare sixty years on, in our own over-cautious day, is another story altogether.

Sade was one of Surrealism's foundational pillars. Another was his spiritual great-grandson, the Montevideo-born poet the Comte de Lautréamont. Lautréamont, who died in 1870 at the age of twenty-four under mysterious circumstances, is mainly remembered as the author of the prose poem *The Cantos of Maldoror.* The narrative, such as it is, follows the picaresque and often hallucinatory adventures of its eponymous anti-hero, who styles himself the personification of evil and who is engaged throughout most of the book with a battle to the death against God, or as he calls him, the Creator (when he isn't calling him worse). *Maldoror* is full of wild invention and grimly exhilarating humor over an underlayer of deep torment; the list of writers, artists, musicians, and filmmakers it influenced stretches from Dalí and Godard to Jim Morrison, John Ashbery, and the Beats. It is also full of what we would now consider child abuse, misogyny, sadism (that word again), animal cruelty, and various other atrocities. No doubt it would have been banned when it was first printed in 1869, had anyone actually noticed its existence at the time.

But then, shortly before his death, the author pulled an about-face. Immediately after celebrating evil in *Maldoror,* Lautréamont—this time under his birth name, Isidore Ducasse—published a slim pamphlet called *Poésies,* consisting of brief aphorisms in prose. On closer examination, it turned out that many of these aphorisms were actually canonical maxims by moralists such as Pascal and La Rochefoucauld, familiar to any French schoolchild, but turned on their heads to celebrate positivity and humanism. Where Pascal, for instance, had written, "Man is only a reed, the weakest in nature . . . a vapor, a drop of water is enough to kill him," Ducasse countered with, "Man is an oak. Nature contains nothing sturdier," and so on. As he announced in a programmatic headnote, "I replace melancholy with courage, doubt with certainty, despair with hope, wickedness with good . . . skepticism with faith."

Many, Ducasse included, have described *Poésies* as a "correction" of *Maldoror*, but we might also see it as a counterpoint. Ducasse began with passion and rage, the sparks needed to light the fire and set revolutions in motion, then continued with the more sober and optimistic reflection needed to bring them to fruition. Faced with the cynicism and the defeatism of his own frenzied fantasies, as well as with the suppression of human grandeur in moralists such as Pascal, Ducasse replaced "despair with hope," offering a lesson of agency and uplift from within the very corpus of repression. Like Rimbaud, whose renunciation of poetry and disappearance into the North African desert sealed his literary reputation, Ducasse's repudiation of his own jet-black apoplexies highlighted both the torment and its negation in an endless dialectical spin-cycle, an enigma forever to be read and pondered, never to be solved.

★

In embracing transgressive figures such as Sade and Lautréamont, the Surrealists were not merely straining for provocative effect. More substantially, the movement promoted itself as one of the great currents of liberation in the twentieth century, the resolute enemy of stifling social and moral conventions, and this extended far beyond literature and art. Its calls, in the 1920s and 1930s, for rethinking the status of women and people of different races, for freedom of imagination and sexuality, and for political revolution directly influenced the protests of May '68 and are not unlike calls that have sounded more and more urgently in recent years. It is also at the origin of many things we now take for granted, from the imagery that we respond to, to the humor that we appreciate, to the sense of strangeness that we unthinkingly call "surreal"; and it laid the groundwork for a larger degree of candor and personal engagement in artistic expression, to which today's productions owe a great deal.

It also established the link between one's moral and aesthetic worth that, until then, had few real equivalents in the European artistic heritage. When Breton posited that poetry "emanates more from the lives of human beings . . . than from what they have written," he was sketching out an ethics of artistic creation that radically reframed the issue. Rather than being judged solely on its own merits, one's art was also answerable to the behavior of its producer—a consideration that resonates even more loudly today in debates over the artistic virtues versus personal vices of figures ranging from Picasso to Louis C.K.

What makes Surrealism such a good case study in this regard is precisely the disparity between the ideals that it promoted and the results that it often delivered, or the behavior that its members displayed. On the one hand, unlike their more sulfuric role models, the Surrealists might vehemently advocate for a positive and synthetic vision: the "point of the mind," as Breton famously put it, "at which life and death, the real and the imagined, past and future, the communicable and the incommunicable, high and low, cease to be perceived as contradictions." But they could also prove just as corrosive as Sade or Lautréamont, and were never shy about expressing their dislikes.

Their early version of "cancel culture" could take various forms, from the twin lists headlined "Read / Don't Read"—the "Don't Reads" being the longer of the two and ending in "etc., etc., etc."—to the so-called trial of Maurice Barrès. A renowned novelist, Barrès had been admired by Breton, Louis Aragon, and other future Surrealists in their formative years as a paragon of personal freedom, the "prince of youth," but with World War I he had hardened into a superpatriot and archconservative. Feeling betrayed, Breton and his friends staged a mock trial of Barrès in May 1921 before a packed house at the Hôtel des Sociétés Savantes, an ornate late-nineteenth-century edifice on the aptly named Rue Danton in Paris' sixth arrondissement. The charge: "conspiracy against the safety of the Mind." When the "court" ultimately handed down a sentence of twenty years' hard labor for Barrès, Breton, who had pushed for the death penalty, was disappointed. Barrès himself, of course, was nowhere near the proceedings and probably couldn't have cared less, but Breton had prosecuted his case with such ferocity that some wondered what might have happened had the defendant been present. (Fifteen years later, they would get their answer from Moscow.)

Much less symbolic were the Surrealists' true cancelations: the periodic exclusions of writers from within their own ranks. In 1926, not long after the movement's founding, several of the original personnel were drummed out of the group for not embracing its turn toward Communist politics. This was followed by other purges over the succeeding years, resulting in the loss of many prominent members, some of whom were pushed to the brink of suicide, or past it, for failings that ranged from practicing hack journalism to political waffling to not condemning vehemently enough those whom the group had condemned. While Surrealism promised many freedoms, the one freedom it apparently could not abide, and toward which Breton could react with remarkable savagery, was the freedom to dissent. In the name of emancipation, it practiced excommunication.

These excommunications were in part a referendum on loyalty—are you with the program or not?—and sometimes simply an outlet for personal spite, but more fundamentally they were an interrogation of identity: you are defined by the company you keep, by both your actions and theirs, and tolerating intolerable elements reflects back on you. Returning to Breton's statement about "poetry emanating from life," what happens when the life no longer lives up to the demands of the poetry? And more to the point, how successfully did Surrealism as a collective live up to its own demands? Three well-documented aspects of Surrealism's engagements in particular—with race, sexuality, and gender—act as a litmus test of how the movement's historical stances might fare against contemporary judgments.

In matters of race, the Surrealists publicly aligned themselves with people of color, denouncing French colonialism and the inequities it fostered at home and abroad. As early as the 1930s, the group was publishing anti-colonialist broadsides and protesting manifestations such as the huge state-sponsored Colonial Exhibition. Under the collaborationist Vichy government of Marshal Pétain, Breton invited the Afro-Cuban artist Wifredo Lam to illustrate one of his books, telling a journalist from the conservative *Le Figaro* that the choice of Lam was meant "to make clear just how sympathetic I am to Marshal Pétain's racist concepts." In 1941, in Martinique, he met and collaborated with the poets Aimé and Suzanne Césaire, future co-founders of the Négritude movement. And in 1946, on a visit to Haiti, Breton told a student audience: "Surrealism is allied with people of color . . . because it has always been on their side against every form of white imperialism and banditry."

At the same time, the movement's antiracism falls short when we consider the relative neglect in the canon of Black Surrealists such as Hector Hippolyte, Hervé Télémaque, René Menil, Léopold Senghor, Jules Monnerot, Pierre Yoyotte, and Ted Joans—and even, to some extent, the Césaires—who only now are receiving serious critical attention. Meanwhile, the most meaningful blend of Surrealism with a specifically Black vision, Afro-surrealism, did not originate with the European Surrealists, but had to develop on its own, independent of them, and with distinct differences. Generally speaking, non-European Surrealist groups, while retaining a greater or lesser identification with the movement, ultimately had to craft a version of Surrealism that spoke to their own cultural realities; whereas the Paris, Brussels, and London groups, even while promoting a broad internationalism, kept their focus on a predominately white European set of references.

When it comes to sex, while Surrealism enjoys a libertine reputation in the popular imagination, all licentiousness all the time, the reality was that these bourgeois young men were rather prudish. Yes, they believed in "free union" and "mad love" and abhorred marriage as an institution (even though many of them were married); and yes, they promoted the idea that a grand passion could excuse anything—though, not surprisingly, that particular freedom usually ran in only one direction. But they were also subject to the prejudices of the era, and quite a few strictures were voiced—particularly by Breton, who pontifically denounced sex workers, multiple partners, promiscuity, women's orgasms, and male homosexuality.

No doubt the most blatant and complex of the Surrealist double-standards concerns the status of women. On the one hand, Surrealism welcomed more women into its ranks than any other art movement of its time—some of them, including Leonora Carrington, Dorothea Tanning, Remedios Varo, Joyce Mansour, Lee Miller, Leonor Fini, Meret Oppenheim, and Kay Sage, now as celebrated as their male counterparts. Within the group, women were honored as muses and creative inspirations, exalted as superior beings attuned to natural and supernatural forces beyond the reach of men, and promised an alternative to the stifling roles that mainstream society expected them to fill. But all too often these grand promises simply fell flat, and the women who came to Surrealism as artists and writers with their own talents and ambitions, or who claimed for themselves the same freedoms in lifestyle and beliefs that the men did, were often disappointed to find themselves facing obstacles from their own peers that hardly differed from those of society at large.

Given the above, it would be tempting to brush away Surrealism as just another exercise that failed to live up to its big claims. But there might be a better way of responding to this: by identifying the moments Surrealism offers in which prohibition becomes opportunity. Rather than repudiating the movement for its failures, the women and the artists of color who gravitated toward it took its promise of emancipation, the energies it liberated, the prospects it enabled, and made them their own. Léopold Senghor once remarked that the poets of Négritude adapted Surrealist tenets to their use, accepting the movement "as a means, but not as an end, as an ally, and not as a master." Because of Surrealism, wrote Suzanne Césaire, "voices that would not be what they are [without it] resound everywhere." The best criticism is neither rejection nor apology, but constant reevaluation and regeneration.

★

What does it mean for the humanities now if art, writings, and philosophies deemed unworthy simply get thrown onto the trash heap of history because they fail to conform to prevailing, and oh so transitory, notions of truth, beauty, or virtue? Where will fruitful challenges originate, if not in studying and debating works that offend and shock, or that fail to keep their promises? Must we "burn" everyone who, in their poetry or their person, does not live up to the ideals that we wish them to embody?

Over the years, as I continued to ponder my philosophical quandary from graduate school, I came to realize that the point of reading literature so closely was to learn how to read the world, that is, the fine print of the world, the signs and underlying messages encoded in people, things, events, exchanges, and surroundings. Paradoxically, given the emphasis on hermetic concentration, what this training really provided was a wider and deeper sensitivity to the context surrounding those people and events. This involved opening my eyes and my mental faculties to ways of thinking and expressing that I had not yet encountered—some of which troubled or upset me, but all of which were crucial steps in my learning how to understand my environments with discernment and broadmindedness.

Sade, Lautréamont, and the Surrealists are problematic because they challenge the values we like to think we celebrate, or because they confront us with frustrations and disappointments; but as such they also open doors toward a meaningful response. They were desperate people living and creating in desperate and pivotal times, whether the French Revolution, the Franco-Prussian War, or the aftermath of World War I. As we live through our own desperate and pivotal era, we might do well to ask what work such as theirs, however removed or outdated it might seem at first, can tell us about our own volatile experience.

One of the most pernicious aspects of our fractious political and cultural landscape—alongside the decimation of our personal liberties, the erosion of civic discourse, governmental paralysis in the face of rising gun violence, and so much else—is the intolerance that it has fostered: not only the caricaturish intolerance for the values of diversity and inclusion that the liberal arts are meant to promote, but a resistance, even a fear—all along the political spectrum—toward engaging with viewpoints that we find alien and distressing, precisely because they *are* alien and distressing. As if we had somehow lost our ability to speak to things that we abhor in other than extreme ways. We demand, we shout, we insist, which is sometimes the necessary response. But what we must not lose is the ability to talk, and more than that, to listen, to weigh, to ponder, to empathize.

If we are to be full-fledged human beings, we must learn the ability to enter into other points of view, including those that antagonize our deepest beliefs. Even as we disagree with or fight them, we must recognize them as human expressions. Saving ourselves from a reality soiled by ever more entrenched parochialism and flattened by defeatism and despair will depend on our capacity to evaluate lucidly, to look beyond buzzwords and bubbles, to see past labels that are often just a surrogate for thinking: there are no surrogates for thinking. It will depend on our ability and our willingness to contemplate the lessons of the humanities with minds wide open, and to interrogate our own and others' beliefs with honesty, compassion, and courage; otherwise, we leave a free entrance to noxious blowhards whose only qualification is to shout louder than anyone else in the room. Knowing how to read the world with an open mind is not just a life hack; it is also a tool for survival.

The Surrealists, for all their obsession with grasping the unconscious, were not particularly known for empathy. While some of their pronouncements, such as Breton's remark about the "point of the mind," might be read as aspirational, they generally preferred to operate in the vituperative register—which some, like Robert Desnos, elevated to a fine art. And yet they knew how to hear, and to hear effectively. Before they went on the attack, they did the necessary work. In 1949, for example, Breton unmasked a forged poem by Rimbaud strictly on the basis of intuitive affinity. His seventy-page pamphlet, *Caught Red-Handed*, takes aim at the literary critics who fell for the hoax (basically all of them), dismantling their arguments point by point in a humiliating show of superior understanding. Not very friendly, perhaps, but in its wounding way more respectful: Breton actively listened to what those critics had to say before delivering his withering refutation. There is a lesson in that. We can, if we must, endure a culture of intellectual incivility; sometimes it might even be beneficial. What we cannot afford, what we must not abide is a culture of intellectual abdication, or, worse, intellectual cowardice.

JUMP CUTS

The opening shot is like something out of a nightmare. A vague nocturnal cityscape in the background, out of focus, barely registered: a dream panorama of San Francisco. Stretched across the screen, suspended in sharp close-up, a horizontal bar, the top rung of a ladder. Instants later, a hand juts up from the bottom of the frame and grips the bar.

The essence of cinema is to make you see what lies outside the frame. In the extreme close-up that kicks off Alfred Hitchcock's *Vertigo* (1958), the tension derives from your being deprived of peripheral vision, having your gaze forced into a particular orientation, directed to a place it doesn't necessarily want to go. Not seeing what surrounds you elicits a shiver of claustrophobia and foreboding, the same foreboding triggered by the phrase "Objects in mirror are closer than they appear": something might be near enough to hurt you, but you don't have enough perspective, enough distance, to recognize it. An extreme close-up is a severe manipulation, pushing subjectivity into the danger zone: the threat that others see but you can't; the projectile about to hit you in the head; the forbidden lover who will be the death of you, but whom you can't resist, can't perceive as harmful.

A hand grips the bar and a man hoists himself onto a rooftop, pursued by a plainclothes detective and a cop in uniform. The felon jumps the gap onto the next roof and keeps running; the patrolman follows suit; the plainclothesman, John "Scottie" Ferguson, slips on the roof tiles and finds himself dangling from a sagging gutter over the alley far below. Paralyzed by vertigo, he cannot grasp his colleague's helping hand, and the patrolman, as in a nightmare, falls screaming into the alley.

★

Why would she do it? Why would Judy Barton, shop assistant, allow herself to be remade into the simulacrum of a dead woman? Why would her older suitor want to remake her? The suitor is Scottie Ferguson (Jimmy Stewart). The dead woman was patrician Madeleine Elster (Kim Novak), whom Scottie, now retired from the police force, had been hired to protect. Did Madeleine's husband, shipping magnate Gavin Elster, hire Scottie because he truly feared that his wife was being driven mad by her grandmother's ghost? Is that why Madeleine killed herself, in a leap from a bell tower? It was Scottie's acute vertigo that kept him from reaching Madeleine in time, just as he couldn't reach for the patrolman's hand on the roof. But the guilt he feels is not simply over another fatality he couldn't prevent; it is also over the death of a woman with whom he had fallen desperately in love. A woman he now tries to bring back to life by recreating her in Judy.

"If you lose me, then you'll know . . . I loved you and wanted to go on loving you": this was Madeleine's final declaration to Scottie, moments before she ran up the mission tower in San Juan Bautista for her fatal jump, while he, clinging to the rickety steps, watched in impotent horror. Tormented by guilt, Scottie suffers a nervous collapse, a nightmare of falling into the void, arms lifting from his sides: a terror so consuming that it lands him in the sanitarium. Later, released and convalescing, he spends his days revisiting the sites of his earlier encounters with Madeleine, seeing her at every turn, still in the grip of a passion that now has no object. Redemption finally seems to come in the form of brassy, auburn-haired Judy—the film's trailer dubs her a "tawdry redhead"—who somehow reminds him of the blonde, ethereal Madeleine. Following Judy back to her hotel, he allays her suspicions and invites her to dinner. Before long, he embarks on a relentless campaign to transform her into his vanished paramour.

The twist, as we soon learn, is that Madeleine and her near doppelgänger are in fact the same woman. In flashback, we relive Madeleine's suicidal flight up the church tower steps, this time discovering that it was actually Judy running up those steps, that Gavin Elster was waiting in the belfry with the strangled body of his actual wife in his arms, and that he threw it from the tower once Judy, as Madeleine, was safely out of Scottie's sight.

At first tempted to leave Scottie a letter of confession and disappear for good ("I was the tool and you the victim of Gavin Elster's plan to murder his wife"), Judy instead resolves to stay and win his affections a second time, for her real self. From this moment on, we know, as Scottie does not, that Judy is none other than the woman he is longing to recreate, and that his frantic attempts to make her over, back into what he thought she had been, can only lead to her undoing.

Why does Judy agree to it? Because, contrary to Elster's carefully scripted plot, she has indeed fallen in love with Scottie, and really does want to go on loving him: "It's not fair. It's too late. It wasn't supposed to happen this way!" she cried in unrehearsed protest before her staged death. Judy does it because she is powerless to resist the lure of spellbinding Scottie once more. And because she, too, has a demon of guilt to exorcise: the guilt of having taken a man she esteemed, whose kind attentions attracted her, and left him broken; the guilt of having helped another man, a calculating killer, ruin the life of one she loved. Perhaps if she is able to build Scottie back up, reincarnate Madeleine in a more salutary and less deceitful form, the form Scottie believed he knew all along, she can redeem them both. She does it, even though it means placing herself in danger: the legal danger of being unmasked as Elster's accomplice; the mortal danger of having to replay the part of

Madeleine for Scottie, who, in his willful obliviousness to Judy's distress, proves even more ruthless than Elster.

And so Judy falls victim to the ghost of the fictionalized Madeleine, just as Elster claimed the real Madeleine had fallen victim to the ghost of her mad ancestor. The suspense lies in wondering not only when and how Scottie will realize his tragic misapprehension, but also whether Judy will let herself be transformed once again, giving one more twist to the Moebius strip of identity and setting the tragedy in motion.

★

"It's an odd thing," Oscar Wilde once quipped, "but everyone who disappears is said to be seen in San Francisco. It must be a delightful city, and possess all the attractions of the next world." By the time of *Vertigo*'s release in 1958, those attractions had changed, and the city had moved firmly into the present world. "The things that spell San Francisco to me are disappearing fast," Gavin Elster muses to Scottie, who is gazing at a large nineteenth-century print of the city on Gavin's office wall. Later still, in 1984, when *Vertigo* was re-released after more than a decade-long absence from circulation, the filmmaker Chris Marker noted that Hitchcock's bird's-eye panoramas of San Francisco already looked as quaint and dated as Elster's etching.*

Despite this, San Francisco remains a city profoundly attentive to, even haunted by, its past, of which *Vertigo* has since become a part—as Charles Barr relates in his British Film Institute monograph on the

---

* Alongside the books cited in this essay, from which much of the background information is drawn, two important resources were Chris Marker's film *Sans soleil* (1983) and his article "A free replay (notes on *Vertigo*)."

film, it has inspired more walking tours and pilgrimages to its locations than any other movie (not to mention a host of cinematic tributes, from Brian De Palma's *Obsession* [1976] to the Mel Brooks spoof *High Anxiety* [1977] to Paul Verhoeven's *Basic Instinct* [1992] to Guy Maddin's SF-centric found-footage reconstruction *The Green Fog* [2017]—we could go on). Hitchcock's daughter, Pat, said that her father considered San Francisco an "American Paris," though *Vertigo*'s loving familiarity with its sights and history are likely due more to longtime resident Samuel Taylor, the movie's principal screenwriter, than to the director.

Walking around the city today, especially with the iconography of *Vertigo* in mind, it's hard not to feel, yet again, that the things spelling San Francisco have continued to disappear. The art gallery in the Palace of the Legion of Honor, where Madeleine sits transfixed before the portrait of her tragic ancestor, Carlotta Valdes, is still there, though the gallery that housed the fictional *Portrait of Carlotta* doesn't look the same. The Theater of the Palace of Fine Arts, near which Scottie and Judy stroll late in the film, can be approached from the same angle, along Baker Street, after descending a vertiginous flight of steps alongside the Presidio; but it is only a reconstruction: the original palace, created for the 1915 Panama-Pacific Exposition, fell into disrepair and was rebuilt in 1965, eight years after *Vertigo* was shot. The Presidio itself, or at least the part of it closest to the Palace of Fine Arts, is now home to a digital arts complex and headquarters of Lucasfilm, replete with "iconic Yoda fountain." Other locations have vanished altogether: Ernie's restaurant, where Scottie first glimpses Madeleine, closed in 1995, a victim of changing culinary tastes; Ransohoff's department store—whose floor manager, trying to accommodate Scottie's finicky requirements for the perfect Madeleine outfit, tartly observes that "the gentleman seems to know what he wants"—suffered the same fate in 1976; and the old Portman Mansion on Gough Street (the film's

McKittrick Hotel, where Madeleine goes to commune with the ghost of Carlotta) was demolished the year after *Vertigo* was released. Still others have become unrecognizable. The Empire Hotel on Sutter Street, where Judy lived after Elster used and abandoned her, was first rebaptized the York Hotel, and today, in a nod to its famous lineage, goes by the name Hotel Vertigo. Scottie's home at 900 Lombard Street (the street that boasts "the crookedest block in the world" just a few yards away), though still the same structure as in the film's exteriors, was covered over in 2012 with a gray "spite wall" that hides the porch on which he checked his mailbox, and the distinctive red chimney has also been painted gray, the house's owners apparently wishing to discourage importunate film buffs. Before this, the metal railings and red front door were concealed behind huge evergreens, leaving them partially visible from the street but still much less inviting than when Madeleine drove up in her green Jaguar to deliver an apology.

What does remain is the impression of eternal height. The upslopes in San Francisco are a source of awe, seeming to loom suddenly in front of you at a sixty-degree angle, as if in a topography-bending dream from Christopher Nolan's *Inception*. From the sidewalks, the houses rise at severe inclines, made even more severe by the steep flights of stairs leading from ground to porch on some of the older structures, and by the fact that so many streets are themselves sharply tilted. The resulting sense of imbalance and dizziness calls to mind the house in another Hitchcock film, *Psycho*; inspired by Edward Hopper's 1925 painting *House by the Railroad*, it conveys a similar feeling of ascent and foreboding.

One could, in fact, characterize *Vertigo* as a fluctuating rhythm of ups and downs, highs and lows, leaps and falls, as well as of accelerated and decelerated tempi. The inclines, the steps in front of the houses, the many shots of Scottie ascending and descending the San Francisco roadways in his DeSoto—all contribute as much to the sense of giddiness and instability as do the characters' emotional peaks and valleys. This is a film of plunging bodies and plunging views (not least, the innovative zoom-in/reverse-tracking shot that simulates Scottie's acrophobia), of heights scaled and depths plumbed. It might just as well have been called *Vertical.*

Moving through *Vertigo* is like moving through an unknown city—or, more accurately, a city you never knew existed (much as Scottie discovers a foreign underside to the San Francisco he thought he'd known all his life). You uncover the city, and the film, in pieces: neighborhoods that don't quite fit together, street grids that don't entirely make sense. You are forced to assemble, piece by piece and episode by episode, a story that might or might not cohere. Watching *Vertigo* is like trying to follow the *Late Late Show* while dozing off: the scenes add up, but not entirely. Like Scottie, you never have the complete picture, until you do.

★

"The power and the freedom." Chris Marker (several of whose works, including his 1962 masterpiece *La Jetée*, contain explicit references to *Vertigo*—as does *12 Monkeys* [1995], Terry Gilliam's homage to Marker's homage) points out that some variant of the phrase occurs three times in the film, spoken by or about three different men who use their power and freedom to cause a woman's downfall: Gavin Elster, regretting the old days of San Francisco while orchestrating his wife's murder; the bookstore owner "Pop" Leibel, speaking of the "rich and powerful man" who seduced and abandoned Carlotta Valdes; and Scottie himself, referring to Gavin, but having forced the same lethal transformation on Judy.

Scottie worries that he has lost *his* power and freedom. Sitting with his old friend Midge (Barbara Bel Geddes), he parries her disapproving questions about why he chose not to stay on the police force after the rooftop tragedy: "You mean, and sit behind a desk, chair-borne?" Midge is Scottie's comfort zone, the only one with enough seniority to call him "John," or "Johnny," or "Johnny-O" ("Old friends call me John, acquaintances call me Scottie," he explains to Madeleine, who prefers the name John but still calls him Scottie), a voice of reason growing ever fainter in this wilderness of intertwined pathologies. Scottie's college sweetheart and fiancée for "three whole weeks," she has settled into the role of faithful, torch-bearing companion, solicitous and motherly, a pal rather than a lover. But it's not only Midge (by definition a "gnat" or "small person"—a pest) who has failed to raise his temperature, for although Scottie is "a big boy," as she archly puts it, we learn early on that he never married, and we have every reason to believe that there has never been a great love in his life. Now, having stared down his own mortality, having discovered his crippling condition and caused another man's death, Scottie peers into the abyss of a solitary existence that no longer enjoys the comfort of professional definition and has never known the vertigo of sexual passion. Midge is not the one for him, for it's clear that she and Scottie can't consummate anything—not their college engagement, not the dinner plans they make and break, not even the drink that he doesn't get to finish as she rushes them both out the door. Their entire relationship is a coitus interruptus.

It's Madeleine, with her profile and her trances, her Mona Lisa smiles and cool demeanor, her inner demons and beguiling terrors, who fits the shape of Scottie's fantasy, the fantasy he didn't even know he had until meeting her. It's the fantasy of like meets like, of another person's hidden damage highlighting and validating your own, the fatal attraction of a beautiful, unbalanced woman crying out for rescue. (Scottie and Madeleine: S+M.) It's the fantasy of a love-swell powerful enough to lift you up and knock you down. The obsession that drives Scottie is born not so much of lust as of dread: the dread of losing his power, of growing old alone, of impotence. Hitchcock blamed *Vertigo*'s lack of success on Jimmy Stewart being "too old" for the part, but it is precisely his age that makes the character poignant, and his fantasy so tragic. Without Madeleine, the fantasy withers and dies, and so does Scottie's capacity for love; without her, he will no longer be able to perform, no longer be able, in common parlance, to get it up.

★

Madeleine dresses up: white coat with scarf and gloves, iridescent emerald shawl over black evening gown, and that elegant, understated gray suit. Judy, in her natural state, dresses down: in lavenders to go out on the town (a choice more consonant with the tastes of Kim Novak, who loved lavender and hated that gray suit), more often in a bottle-green skirt-and-sweater combo that, especially in comparison to Madeleine's emerald satins, merely looks cheap. But Scottie, for all his attention to her clothes, isn't really interested in dress at all, as his director was fully aware. "Cinematically," Hitchcock commented, "all of [Jimmy] Stewart's efforts to re-create the dead woman are shown in such a way that he seems to be trying to undress her, instead of the other way around . . . [Later, he] is disappointed because she hasn't put her hair up in a bun. What this really means is that the girl has almost stripped, but she still won't take her knickers off . . . What Stewart is really waiting for is for the woman to emerge totally naked this time, and ready for love." For the crucial scene in question, in which Judy has finally been transformed back into the lost Madeleine, she was originally supposed to make the ultimate adjustment to her hair in front of Scottie, as he watched. A last-minute script revision put that transformation out of his sight and ours, making the revived Madeleine's emergence more dramatic—more like Venus emerging naked from the waters.

Still, in a way, Scottie has already gotten his wish. Earlier, during his initial surveillance, he rescued Madeleine after she jumped into San Francisco Bay, then brought the unconscious woman back to his apartment to recover. She woke in Scottie's bed to find that she'd been undressed so that her clothes could hang up to dry. (We know this from a pan across the apartment, showing the dress hanging from a cupboard in the kitchen. Originally the shot also showed her undergarments, but the censors nixed that detail.) The next day, she returns to Scottie's apartment to deliver "a formal thank-you note" and "a great big apology" for having forced him to dive in after her. "The whole thing must have been so embarrassing for you," she commiserates. "Not at all," he hastens to reassure her. "I enjoyed . . ."—catching himself—". . . talking to you." "I enjoyed talking to *you*," she replies, with a knowing smirk. It is one of the film's rare forays into the register of deliciously low comedy, a breather from the diction of high tragedy that regains the upper hand soon after.

The tragedy is that Scottie can't see what is plainly in front of him; can't countenance Midge's healthy skepticism of Gavin's ghost story, or her "stupid! stupid! stupid!" attempt to insert herself into his bewitchment by pastiching the *Portrait of Carlotta*, replacing the original sitter's face with her own bespectacled visage; can't see through the distracting theater that Elster and Judy-as-Madeleine have staged for his detriment. Scottie is a detective: his determination to make sense of chaos, to rationalize an irrational situation, is an occupational hazard. The irony is that this situation *does* make sense, but a very different sense from what his manipulated, befogged mind has managed to piece together. "You see? There's an answer for everything," he tries to persuade Madeleine, with mounting vehemence. And in fact, there is one—but Scottie's normally acute brain can't pierce the veil of the plot until the very end, when it's too late.

⋆

Even at his highest pitch of anticipation, when Judy-as-Madeleine *rediviva* emerges from the bath of her modest room in the Empire Hotel, painstakingly costumed, made up, dyed, and coiffed in an exact replica of the replica she had once been; even at this crescendo of fulfillment, when to Scottie's wondering eyes his lost love rises from the grave and comes to him for the consummate kiss, before the whole house of cards comes crashing down—even then, there is a flaw, a crack in the facade. It's her smile. The timid look of hope, of wanting to please, of insecurity that after everything she has done she still hasn't done enough, that she is still making a mistake—that timid look is itself the mistake. "It was so real to me," recalled Kim Novak, whose demanding dual role as Madeleine/Judy garnered reviews as diametrically opposed as the two women's personalities, "the coming out and wanting approval in that scene. It was like, is this what you want? Is this what you want from me? My whole body was trembling . . . It was the ultimate defining moment of anybody when they're going to someone they love and they just want to be perfect for them." Only at the very end, back in the bell tower, as she's pleading with Scottie for her life, with a real desperation that mirrors the simulated desperation of her earlier role, does Judy truly look and sound like Madeleine again. And again she must die.

Madeleine's allure comes not only from her polished appearance, "the manner and the words, and those beautiful phony trances," but from a patina of aloofness, a certain haughtiness, which makes her occasional breakdowns ("Scottie! I'm not mad! I'm not mad! I don't want to die!") all the more seductive. She is—at least in her first, invented incarnation—very much to the manor born, fully in control even in her distress, and anything but timid. To this Workaday Johnny-O, ex-cop of "fairly independent" means, she is the Great Unattainable, deserving of worship because so high above him.

The look of humble, dependent hope on Judy's face as she emerges from the bathroom is the big giveaway, a clear sign—clearer even than the necklace that soon afterward blares out the truth—that she will never be Madeleine and that Madeleine was never more than Judy. The Madeleine with whom Scottie has fallen hopelessly in love, who leads him on a citywide game of hide-and-seek that is very much a courtship, full of stolen glimpses and hesitations, dodges and feints (and faints)—*that* Madeleine is a woman who never was. Or at most, as Donald Spoto puts it in *The Art of Alfred Hitchcock*, she is an "unrealized aspect" of Judy, the alluring sophisticate latent inside the tawdry shopgirl. As for the redone Judy, despite the scrupulously reproduced clothes and hair, she is still just a bargain-basement knock-off—and all the more real and loveable for it, since the Madeleine she is now being made to play is at least capable of genuine emotion. But Scottie, watching her emerge from the bath, is too blinded by his own starry-eyed longing to appreciate the differences, or the true similarities.

He *had* noticed them, earlier, when his reconstructive mania was in its first stages. "When we first started out, it was so good," Judy cried in anguish. "We had fun. And then you started in on the clothes." (A curious outburst, given that they've apparently known each other for only a few days—but emotions evolve quickly in Hitchcockland.)

Scottie, in response, recognized that something about her transcended his attempts at a makeover. "It's you, too," he said. "There's something in you . . ." But that "something" remained elusive, and the only way Scottie knew how to reach it was to keep on with the clothes, and the hair, and the makeup . . .

What he was trying to bridge, in those first-starting-out days, was a serious gap in his feelings toward the two women, a gap that becomes plain in the scene where Judy is at home with Scottie, as earlier Madeleine had been after he rescued her from San Francisco Bay. As he had with Madeleine, Scottie gives Judy something to drink (coffee for the refined Madeleine, brandy for the plebeian Judy: "Drink this down. Just like medicine"). And as he had with Madeleine, he invites Judy to sit by the fire. But whereas he had carefully arranged two pillows on the floor for Madeleine to sit on, with Judy he casually drops a single pillow in front of the fireplace. Is he even conscious of the difference in treatment? She, without a doubt, is.

Why does he do it? Why does Scottie hold back from giving in to Judy yet remain fatally attached? One reason is that Scottie has fallen in love not with Madeleine but with her death—the death foreshadowed in the *folie à deux* of her ancestral haunting and, better still, her supposed suicide. What keeps him captive is the mesmerizing dance of Thanatos and Eros. A woman squarely on this side of the life/death schism, someone with ordinary needs and desires, a workaday gal, a Midge, could never hold his attention; but someone constantly on the verge of annihilation—that's another story. Under those conditions, at last, the erotic fixation of his guilt (over the dead policeman, or something else?) can become all-consuming.

Catatonic at St. Joseph's sanitarium after his nervous breakdown, Scottie is diagnosed as suffering from "acute melancholia, together with a guilt complex." But what the doctor doesn't get is that Scottie is content in his melancholy, for never will he love Madeleine as much as when mired in it—just as he'll never truly love Judy until she plummets off the bell tower for the last time. Judy's death frees him to fuse the two women in his heart and finally embrace her, in an orgasm of loss and self-recrimination, for however much of a life he has left.

⋆

By most accounts, Scottie's longing to refashion Judy into his idealized dead blonde is a stand-in for Hitchcock's yearning to create a new blonde star conforming to *his* idealized image. Words like "longing," "yearning," and "aching" come up frequently in discussions of *Vertigo*, and with good reason: behind this ostensible crime thriller is perhaps the most intimate self-portrait Hitchcock ever created, full of buried passions and unconfessed wants. Samuel Taylor recalled that "this was a very important project for Hitch . . . he was feeling this story very deeply, very personally." The uncharacteristic paucity of humor, the pervasive atmosphere of grief, bespeak the broodings of a director who has lain awake on many a dark night.

Vertigo was conceived in 1956, the same year Hitchcock "lost" his favorite actress, protégée, and object of ill-concealed desire, Grace Kelly, to Prince Rainier of Monaco (who, perhaps not coincidentally, bore some resemblance to Tom Helmore's Gavin Elster). Scottie's Pygmalionic way of pushing Judy closer and closer to his necrophiliac fantasy recalls Hitchcock's molding of the bright blonde Kelly over the course of their three films together, as well as his subsequent failures to reincarnate her in other actresses—Vera Miles, Kim Novak, Eva Marie Saint—after her defection. ("I'm very happy that Grace has found herself such a good part," was his dismissive quip on Kelly's marriage.) The blondness of *Vertigo*'s heroine, in fact, seems to have been an essential point from the start: though the process of adapting Pierre Boileau and Thomas Narcejac's novel *D'entre les morts* (1954) took many months and several rounds of scriptwriters, at the very outset Hitchcock changed the fictional Madeleine's "dark hair discreetly tinted with henna" to platinum blonde, leaving the reddish-brown locks to prosaic, workaday Judy.

The year 1956 also saw the release of Hitchcock's previous film with Jimmy Stewart, *The Man Who Knew Too Much*, co-starring blonde girl-next-door Doris Day. Between that and *Vertigo*, Hitchcock's and Stewart's final collaboration, came only the downbeat black-and-white pseudo-documentary *The Wrong Man* (1957), with Henry Fonda and Vera Miles, who initially was the front-runner for the role of Madeleine. The commonly heard story is that Miles, whom Hitchcock had anointed as Kelly's successor in his pantheon of blondes, ruined her chances for super-stardom by getting pregnant shortly before shooting was to begin. But there is ample evidence that Hitchcock was also dissatisfied with her screen tests and concluded early on that he needed an actress with more visceral appeal to convince audiences of Scottie's obsession.

Looking at *Vertigo* today, I find it hard to imagine anyone other than Kim Novak in the role—not Vera Miles or Grace Kelly, not Lana Turner (whom Hitchcock originally considered) or Audrey Hepburn (who reportedly was interested in the part). It is the smoldering darkness underlying Novak's portrayal that lets us fathom Scottie's ruinous attraction to both the ethereal Madeleine and the earthier Judy. No doubt this quality owes something to her instinctive understanding of her dual character, for the transformation of Judy into someone she once was but never *truly* was, and her desire for love and acceptance on her own terms, seem to have resonated as deeply for Novak as Scottie's obsession did for Hitchcock. "When I read [Judy's] lines, 'I want you to love me for me,' I just identified with it so much," she later said. "It was what I felt when I came to Hollywood as a young girl. You know, they want to make you over completely . . . So I related to the resentment of being made over and to the need for approval and the desire to be loved. I really identified with the story because to me it was saying, Please, see who I am. Fall in love with me, not a fantasy."

But how often do we fall in love with people as they really are? Isn't every love object remodeled to fit our expectations and fantasies? Doesn't the object, wittingly or unwittingly, adapt and change to meet those fantasies? And doesn't falling in love sometimes mean falling into a fiction, a masquerade?

After a lifetime of emotional celibacy, Scottie finds his perfect soulmate, and she's a fake; in trying to recreate her, he produces only the counterfeit of a counterfeit, as if the double negative could somehow add up to a genuine positive. Looked at from this perspective, *Vertigo* is not so much about Scottie's consuming desire to possess a dead woman, or Hitchcock's attempt to replace Grace Kelly, or Kim Novak's need to be loved for herself, but about the universally understood quest for a passion that is, by its very nature, unattainable. It is a portrait of pure, unrequited, insatiable, unfulfillable, unresolvable longing. As much as any sonnet or ode, *Vertigo* is a great poetic exploration of how we ache for the resurrection of a love lost and never had.

⋆

Although Boileau and Narcejac wrote *D'entre les morts* (literally, "from among the dead" or "between the dead") with a Hitchcock adaptation in mind, there are a number of significant differences between it and *Vertigo*, nearly all of which point up Hitchcock's mastery at improving a story. (He'd done so several times before, most compellingly when he transformed John Buchan's plodding *The Thirty-Nine Steps* into one of the first great British thrillers.) While the plot is basically the same—ex-cop Flavières is hired by old acquaintance Gévigne to watch over his wealthy wife, Madeleine; the "job" is really a ruse whose purpose is to give Gévigne an alibi for Madeleine's murder; later, Flavières becomes involved with Renée, who turns out to be Madeleine—the change in time and place, from World War II–era Paris to late-fifties San Francisco, gives the film a much different atmosphere and plangency than the source text. The novel, moreover, makes only passing mention of Flavières's debilitating condition, whereas the film gives it titular status (though not without a struggle: the studio, fearing that no one would know what "vertigo" meant, kept trying to force alternate titles on Hitchcock).

Some of the biggest disparities involve the characters, especially the main protagonist. Flavières is self-centered, alcoholic, and ultimately homicidal. When he learns of the plot from Renée, he strangles her in a rage—even though, perversely, he had hounded her for that very admission, having been convinced from the start that Renée was Madeleine. Scottie, for whom this realization is the cold slap that brings him back to reality, is a more tortured antihero. Although in the final account he isn't as different from his French counterpart as it might seem (his fantasy *is* self-centered, he drinks more heavily as the film progresses, and he leads Judy to her death), his reluctant attraction and muted emotional affect make him a much better mirror for our ambivalence than the obnoxious and shallow Flavières, who is merely a "type." Paradoxically, it is fat, greasy Gévigne who comes off as comparatively sympathetic in the novel: his desperate plot to kill his wife seems more morose than Machiavellian, and he doesn't live long enough to enjoy its evil fruits. By contrast, Gavin Elster (German for "magpie"; birds, of any feather, never bode well in Hitchcock) is suave and self-assured: the gentleman knows what he wants.

Another important change is that the denouement, which occurs at the end of the novel, comes much earlier in the movie. This was not part of the original plan: the first two screen treatments (by many hands, including Maxwell Anderson, Alec Coppell, and Hitchcock's old collaborator Angus MacPhail) follow the novel in saving the revelation for the final scene. Only in the third treatment, by Samuel Taylor, are we let in on the secret as soon as Judy enters the story. Taylor's main credit before *Vertigo* was as author of the Broadway hit *Sabrina Fair*, the basis for Billy Wilder's 1954 film. It was he who introduced the character of Midge (Flavières has no such confidante), and it was he who insisted most vehemently that the audience should learn the truth well before Scottie does. As he saw it, keeping viewers in the dark would burden the climactic scene of Scottie's realization with complicated exposition, whereas letting them in on the secret would make them wonder, with mounting anxiety, how long it will take Scottie to discover the truth.

Hitchcock himself was of two minds, and after having shot and edited the revelation flashback he cut it from the release prints, leading to heated disputes with some of his principal collaborators. Disappointing critical response to the previews and an angry phone call from the president of Paramount (who had liked the version with the flashback) persuaded him to reverse his decision, and release prints had to be recalled from distribution so that the footage could be reinserted. Several years later, in his interview with François Truffaut, Hitchcock took credit for the flashback. "Everyone around me was against [the early giveaway]," he said. "They all felt that the revelation should be saved for the end of the picture." Having in the interim become the celebrated auteur of *North by Northwest*, *Psycho*, and *The Birds*, he no doubt felt entitled to rewrite history a little.

★

Hitchcock's films have often been cited for their logical inconsistencies and plot holes, the scenes that seem to be there only for cinematic effect, the moments of disconnect that give the whole the feeling of a dream. (Would Phillip Vandamm really need to lure Roger Thornhill miles out of town and hire a crop duster just to bump him off? Could Gavin Elster really have launched his intricate murder plot in the short time between reading of Scottie's debilitating condition and their first contact?) In this vein, some critics have theorized that the entire storyline of *Vertigo*, after the opening scene, takes place in Scottie's head during his final moments of life, as he hangs from the collapsing gutter—much as Peyton Farquhar in Ambrose Bierce's "An Occurrence at Owl Creek Bridge" fantasizes his escape and reunion with his wife instants before he drops through the gallows. (Bierce, bard of San Francisco's "gay old bohemian days," whose dark spirit presides over *Vertigo*'s perverse twists and turns. Taylor signed the first draft of his screenplay "Samuel Taylor and Ambrose Bierce.") But this reading of the film robs it of its most disturbing message, which is that life *is* irrational and uncontrollable, that we *are* prey to obsessions we can never satisfy. The critic Robin Wood argues that one reason for *Vertigo*'s staying power is that it represents the world in a way we all too readily understand, as "quicksand, unstable, constantly shifting . . . into which we may sink at any step in any direction, illusion and reality constantly ambiguous, even interchangeable." And he goes on to write that "in complexity and subtlety, in emotional depth, in its power to disturb, in the centrality of its concerns, *Vertigo* can as well as any film be taken to represent the cinema's claims to be treated with the respect accorded to the longer established art forms."

That's a retrospective judgment: *Vertigo* earned no such accolades upon its initial release. Instead, it was largely dismissed as "far-fetched nonsense" and "another Hitchcock-and-bull story" (to quote two reviews), while subsequent critics simply ignored it in favor of the splashier successes that immediately followed in the Master's catalogue. Hitchcock himself gives *Vertigo* comparatively short shrift in his conversations with Truffaut, merely expressing regret that it didn't have more impact. It wasn't until the 1984 rerelease that it began to acquire a reputation as Hitchcock's masterpiece, and not until 2012 that it was named the "greatest film of all time" in the prestigious British Film Institute/*Sight & Sound* poll, knocking *Citizen Kane* off the perch it had occupied for fifty years. (In 2022, *Vertigo* was in turn knocked off the perch by Chantal Akerman's 1975 film *Jeanne Dielman, 23 quai du Commerce, 1080 Bruxelles*).

Polls, needless to say, are as arbitrary as anything else, and many viewers prefer the more polished charms of *Rear Window* (in which Jimmy Stewart plays the crusty but loveable photographer L. B. Jeffries) and *The Man Who Knew Too Much* (in which he's the crusty but upstanding doctor Ben McKenna) to *Vertigo*, whose uncomfortably personal quality and problematic hero continue to disorient even ardent fans of Hitchcock's work. Assessing *Vertigo*'s stature in a #MeToo world, David Thomson, in the *London Review of Books*, is damning: "It's irrefutably clear that *Vertigo* is a confession to the damage done by men's grooming of women's desirability. And even if the film is tragic, and even if Novak's performance more and more seems brave or poignant, I don't think its fantasy can go unchastised." While taking Thomson's point, I can't help but nod in agreement at this observation by film historian Dan Auiler in *Vertigo: The Making of a Hitchcock Classic*: "*Vertigo* is not the perfect, pure cinema of *Rear Window*. Yet who is haunted, dogged, pursued by *Rear Window*?" If, as Hitchcock remarked early in his career, the "basis of cinema's appeal is emotional," then few films are as basic as this cry from the depths.

★

Vertigo. Disorientation. Double vision. This is a film of repetitions, reflections, symmetries, mirrors, from the one framing Madeleine at the Podesta Baldocchi flower shop as Scottie watches her buy a nosegay to the one in the hotel room where he notices Carlotta's necklace on Judy's throat. "*All* the gestures, looks, phrases in *Vertigo* have a double meaning," writes Chris Marker. Everything in the film finds its echo, from settings to actions to lines of dialogue. "Madeleine, try! Try for me!" Scottie urges the woman in San Juan Bautista. "Try, Johnny!" says Midge to the dumbly passive Scottie in St. Joseph's sanatorium. "No, it's too late!" Madeleine shouts before her apparent fall. "It's too late. It's too late. There's no bringing her back," moans Scottie moments before Judy falls to her actual death. As Spoto notes, the Spirograph vortices of the title sequence are repeated in the swirls of Madeleine's hair bun (itself a copy of Carlotta's distinctive coif), and the gesture of arranging that hair is itself called to our attention twice: by Madeleine in Scottie's apartment, by Scottie in his quest to recreate her in Judy. Practically Scottie's first and last glimpses of the woman are framed by empty churches: Mission Dolores, where he follows her into the graveyard; the bell tower at San Juan Bautista, where he chases her to her grave. Both at the churchyard and in Judy's final emergence from the bath after her retransformation into Madeleine, she is swathed in a greenish haze. With the logic of a nightmare, places appear and then reappear: Ernie's restaurant, the Legion of Honor museum, the fatal bell-tower steps. Madeleine, followed by Scottie out of professional obligation, appears in the window of the McKittrick Hotel; Judy, followed by him out of nascent obsession, appears in the window of the Empire Hotel. The list goes on.

But ultimately these are just failed repetitions, stunt doubles, further proof that mirrors reflect only what we wish to see. For me, the most affecting part of *Vertigo*, the one that most encapsulates its yearning, is the brief series of shots leading to Scottie's first glimpse of Judy. It serves as the hinge between the melodrama of the first half, detailing Scottie's love and loss of Madeleine, his breakdown and withdrawal, and the second half, with its cruel denouement.

Released from St. Joseph's, Scottie listlessly revisits the sites of his encounters with Madeleine, trying to recapture those heady days that took him from reluctant first look to hopeless infatuation. He lurks about the Brocklebank Apartments on Nob Hill, where the Elsters lived and his journey began; he goes to the Legion of Honor, to the gallery where he first watched Madeleine gazing enraptured at Carlotta's portrait; he returns to Ernie's, the restaurant where she first appeared to him in classic profile, and stands awkwardly by the door for a moment, as if unable to go inside. Each time, the dead Madeleine seems to materialize in front of him before resolving into someone else, some lesser woman. Only in the last instance, when Scottie sees Judy at Podesta Baldocchi and unconsciously rediscovers that classic profile, does the counterfeit have enough authenticity to draw him on.

"You're my second chance, Judy! You're my second chance!" Scottie cries in mingled hope and desolation. But as another famous obsessive, Jay Gatsby, found to his undoing, you can't repeat the past, and there are no second chances. For all his hopefulness, Scottie's revisitations occur only in degraded form. In the first, ascendant phase of his encounters with Madeleine, these places were loci of discovery, creation, belief; in the second, lowered and debased, they are merely scenes of disillusionment, of Scottie's vain bid to relive something that grows deader with each failed attempt, each disappointing excursion. Perhaps more than any other moment in the film, it is this brief sequence of frustrated vignettes that drives home the tragic sadness underlying *Vertigo*, the sense of loss that can never be recovered, time that can never be regained, a past that haunts you but that can never be recaptured, and that never truly existed.

★

The final chapter of *Vertigo* may be the most claustrophobic forty minutes in all of cinema. Charles Barr observes that when Midge, who has just tried in vain to wrest Scottie from his "acute melancholia" with megadoses of Mozart, walks out of St. Joseph's and out of the film, she takes with her the last human presence not involved in the "extraordinarily intense psychodrama" between Scottie and Judy. From this point on, the film belongs almost entirely to the two of them. It is like the first days of an ardent love affair—exhilarating, all-consuming, airless. Soon after their meeting, Scottie begins his suffocating attempts to recast Judy as Madeleine, which lead to her gradual, agonized resignation and their lovemaking. But no sooner has Scottie finally possessed his fantasy-made-flesh than a glimpse of Carlotta's distinctive necklace, which Judy has carelessly donned in her postcoital flush, tells him what we already know.

In a controlled rage, he drives Judy back to San Juan Bautista, the site of Madeleine's putative suicide ("I have to go back into the past once more . . . I need you to be Madeleine for a while. And when it's done, we'll both be free"), and drags her up the same bell-tower steps he couldn't climb the first time. Judy, with rising panic, protests her love: "I was safe when you found me. There was nothing that you could prove . . . I walked into danger and let you change me because I loved you . . . Keep me safe. Please!" But it's too late: there really is no bringing her back. When she tumbles from the narrow ledge, startled by a nun's sudden rise into the belfry, she is already as dead as the discarded body of the real Madeleine. Once again Madeleine dies. Once again Scottie is powerless to prevent it. Once again he is the unwitting instrument of her destruction. Tragedy repeats as greater tragedy.

Inevitable as this ending seems, Hitchcock shot an alternate one, which takes place at some later date, in Midge's apartment. The radio announces that Gavin Elster is being sought in Europe by the police. Moments afterward, a despondent-looking Scottie walks in, Midge pours him a drink, and neither says a word. (Does the fact that she's wearing a bathrobe signal that they have finally settled after all these years and married, or at least consummated their tepid relationship?) This ending, considered a cheap tack-on by most fans, was in fact part of the original script, though Hitchcock's notes on the rough cut suggest that it was shot mainly as a sop to the censors and never meant to be part of the finished film. In any case, as any admirer of *Vertigo* knows, there is only one possible ending. "That final, shocking image of Scottie alone in the tower," writes Dan Auiler, "is what seals the heart and our fate—what binds us to the film, brings us back to countless screenings, drags us to the locations to walk their steps like hungry ghosts." Scottie, in these last, abrupt frames, is a man with nothing more to lose. A man with nowhere to go but down.

On the horizontal ledge he stands bereft, staring at his twice-dead lover below, his face registering the cost of his unrelenting compulsion. The implication is that he's about to follow Judy into the void, or else plunge yet again into melancholia, this time irretrievably. His hands rise slowly from his sides, assuming the same position as on the falling silhouette in his nightmare. Does he fall? We'll never know. A soundtrack crescendo and a final blackout freeze him there, caught for all eternity in the space between the dead.

Acknowledgments

A number of these essays, written over the past three decades, have been lightly (or not so lightly) revised and updated for the present volume, though their substance remains the same. They were originally published in:

"Profound Occultation": *Parnassus* 30:1-2 (spring 2008). "Patabiographical": *Bookforum* (Dec./Jan. 2012). "Love in Vain": *The New Republic* (June 7, 2004). "Through a Glass, Amorously": Booklet essay to the Criterion edition of Jean Cocteau's *Orpheus* (2011). "A Child's Garden of Eccentricities": Introduction to Raymond Roussel, *Impressions of Africa* (Dalkey Archive Press, 2011). "'Love and Theft'": *Parnassus* 34:1-2 (spring 2015). "The Complicated Little Girl": *London Review of Books* (Nov. 28, 1996, as "Dirty's Story"). "Which Year at Where?": Booklet essay to the Criterion edition of Alain Resnais's *Last Year at Marienbad* (2009). "Whoever Is with Me Is Against Me": *The New Republic* (April 9, 2008, as "The Smirk"). "Lives Behind Lives": *Biography and Source Studies*, vol. 5, ed. Frederick R. Karl (New York: AMS Press, 2000). "Art of the Inane": previously unpublished. "Surrealism's Children": *Liberties* 3:1 (fall 2022). "Jump Cuts": *Parnassus* 35:1-2 (summer 2019).

My thanks to the following individuals for commissioning the pieces or for helpful insights in their gestation: Jacky Colliss Harvey, Ben Downing, Liz Helfgott, Frederick R. Karl, Herbert Leibowitz, Christopher Lyon, John O'Brien, David O'Neill, William Rodarmor, Leon Wieseltier, Trevor Winkfield, and Bill Zavatsky; and to Ben Estes and Alan Felsenthal of The Song Cave for the opportunity to revisit them.

OTHER TITLES FROM THE SONG CAVE:

1. *A Dark Dreambox of Another Kind* by **Alfred Starr Hamilton**
2. *My Enemies* by **Jane Gregory**
3. *Rude Woods* by **Nate Klug**
4. *Georges Braque and Others* by **Trevor Winkfield**
5. *The Living Method* by **Sara Nicholson**
6. *Splash State* by **Todd Colby**
7. *Essay Stanzas* by **Thomas Meyer**
8. *Illustrated Games of Patience* by **Ben Estes**
9. *Dark Green* by **Emily Hunt**
10. *Honest James* by **Christian Schlegel**
11. *M* by **Hannah Brooks-Motl**
12. *What the Lyric Is* by **Sara Nicholson**
13. *The Hermit* by **Lucy Ives**
14. *The Orchid Stories* by **Kenward Elmslie**
15. *Do Not Be a Gentleman When You Say Goodnight* by **Mitch Sisskind**
16. *HAIRDO* by **Rachel B. Glaser**
17. *Motor Maids across the Continent* by **Ron Padgett**
18. *Songs for Schizoid Siblings* by **Lionel Ziprin**
19. *Professionals of Hope: The Selected Writings of* **Subcomandante Marcos**
20. *Fort Not* by **Emily Skillings**
21. *Riddles, Etc.* by **Geoffrey Hilsabeck**
22. *CHARAS: The Improbable Dome Builders* by **Syeus Mottel** (Co-published with Pioneer Works)
23. *YEAH NO* by **Jane Gregory**

24. *Nioque of the Early-Spring* by **Francis Ponge**
25. *Smudgy and Lossy* by **John Myers**
26. *The Desert* by **Brandon Shimoda**
27. *Scardanelli* by **Friederike Mayröcker**
28. *The Alley of Fireflies and Other Stories* by **Raymond Roussel**
29. *CHANGES: Notes on Choreography* by **Merce Cunningham** (Co-published with the Merce Cunningham Trust)
30. *My Mother Laughs* by **Chantal Akerman**
31. *Earth* by **Hannah Brooks-Motl**
32. *Everything and Other Poems* by **Charles North**
33. *Paper Bells* by **Phan Nhiên Hạo**
34. *Photographs: Together & Alone* by **Karlheinz Weinberger**
35. *A Better Place Is Hard to Find* by **Aaron Fagan**
36. *Rough Song* by **Blanca Varela**
37. *In the Same Light: 200 Poems for Our Century From the Migrants & Exiles of the Tang Dynasty,* translated by **Wong May**
38. *On the Mesa: An Anthology of Bolinas Writing (50th Anniversary Edition)*, edited by **Ben Estes and Joel Weishaus**
39. *Listen My Friend, This Is the Dream I Dreamed Last Night* by **Cody-Rose Clevidence**
40. *Poetries* by **Georges Schehadé**
41. *Wings in Time* by **Callie Garnett**
42. *Two Murals* by **Jesús Castillo**
43. *Punks: New & Selected Poems* by **John Keene**
44. *ABC Moonlight* by **Ben Estes**
45. *Star Lake* by **Arda Collins**
46. *The Maybe-Bird* by **Jennifer Elise Foerster**
47. *Seriously Well* by **Helge Torvund**

48. *Dereliction* by **Gabrielle Octavia Rucker**

49. *Bookworm: Conversations with* **Michael Silverblatt**

50. *April* by **Sara Nicholson**

51. *Valley of the Many-Colored Grasses* by **Ronald Johnson**

52. *The Sphinx and the Milky Way: Selections from the Notebooks of* **Charles Burchfield**

53. *Telling the Truth as It Comes Up: Selected Talks & Essays 1991–2018* by **Alice Notley**

54. *Lunar Solo: Selected Poems* by **Jules Laforgue**

55. *Stranger* by **Emily Hunt**

56. *The Selkie* by **Morgan Võ**

57. *Hereafter* by **Alan Felsenthal**

58. *Cold Dogs* by **Zan de Parry**

59. *Saturday* by **Margaret Ross**

60. *Many Poems* by **Roberta Iannamico**

61. *Ultraviolet of the Genuine* by **Hannah Brooks-Motl**

62. *Silkworm's Pansori* by **David Seung**

63. *Tantrums in Air* by **Emily Skillings**